NEED to KNOW

Key facts at your fingertips

AQA A-LEVEL PE

Kirk Bizley

Ross Howitt

HODDER
EDUCATION
AN HACHETTE UK COMPANY

Hachette UK's policy is to use papers that are natural, renewable and recyclable products and made from wood grown in well-managed forests and other controlled sources. The logging and manufacturing processes are expected to conform to the environmental regulations of the country of origin.

Orders: please contact Hachette UK Distribution, Hely Hutchinson Centre, Milton Road, Didcot, Oxfordshire, OX11 7HH. Telephone: 01235 827827. Email: education@hachette.co.uk

Lines are open from 9 a.m. to 5 p.m., Monday to Friday. You can also order through our website: www. hoddereducation.co.uk

ISBN: 978 1 5104 2857 7

© Kirk Bizley and Ross Howitt

First published in 2018 by

Hodder Education,
An Hachette UK Company
Carmelite House
50 Victoria Embankment
London EC4Y 0DZ

Impression number   10 9 8 7 6 5 4 3 2

Year   2022 2021

Typeset in India by Aptara Inc.

Printed and bound by CPI Group (UK) Ltd, Croydon, CR0 4YY

A catalogue record for this title is available from the British Library.

Contents

Getting the most from this book

This *Need to Know* guide is designed to help you throughout your course as a companion to your learning and a revision aid in the months or weeks leading up to the final exams.

The following features in each section will help you get the most from the book.

You need to know

Each topic begins with a list summarising what you 'need to know' in this topic for the exam.

Exam tip

Key knowledge you need to demonstrate in the exam, tips on exam technique, common misconceptions to avoid and important things to remember.

Key terms

Definitions of highlighted terms in the text to make sure you know the essential terminology for your subject.

Do you know?

Questions at the end of each topic to test you on some of its key points. Check your answers here: www.hoddereducation.co.uk/needtoknow/answers

Synoptic links

Reminders of how knowledge and skills from different topics in your A-level relate to one another.

End of section questions

Questions at the end of each main section of the book to test your knowledge of the specification area covered. Check your answers here: www.hoddereducation.co.uk/needtoknow/answers

1 Applied anatomy and physiology

1.1 Cardio-respiratory and cardiovascular systems

You need to know
- impact of physical activity and sport on the health and fitness of the individual
- hormonal, neural and chemical regulation of responses during physical activity and sport
- receptors involved in the regulation of responses during physical activity
- transportation of oxygen, including venous return, Starling's law of the heart, cardiovascular drift and arterio-venous oxygen difference (A-VO$_2$ diff)

Impact of physical activity

One of the major impacts of physical activity is on the heart. Physical activity helps to strengthen the heart muscle and increases the size of the left ventricle.

In addition to a stronger heart muscle, physical activity can also help to:
- reduce the potential incidence of heart disease
- prevent or reduce high blood pressure — high blood pressure can be a health risk as there is a higher force exerted against the blood vessel wall
- reduce the adverse effects of high cholesterol levels — high levels of 'bad' cholesterol can increase the risk of heart disease
- reduce the likelihood/incidence of a stroke

Physical activity will help to develop the fitness of an individual. One reason is the effect on cardiac output — for both trained and untrained individuals. Cardiac output ($\dot{Q}$) is stroke volume (SV) × heart rate (HR). Cardiac output increases during exercise due to an increase in stroke volume and an increase in heart rate (see Table 1).

Key terms

Blood pressure The force exerted against the blood vessel wall, often referred to as blood flow × resistance, measured as a comparison of systolic (contracting) pressure over diastolic (relaxing/filling) pressure

Cholesterol A waxy, fat-like substance in the blood and cells of the body

Stroke This occurs when the blood supply to the brain is cut off, causing damage to the brain cells

Cardiac output The volume of blood pumped out by the heart ventricles per minute

Stroke volume The volume of blood pumped out by the heart ventricles in each contraction

Table 1 Cardiac output in a trained and untrained individual

	stroke volume × heart rate = cardiac output (SV × HR = Q)
During exercise: untrained person	120 ml × 202 = 24.24 litres
During exercise: trained person	170 ml × 202 = 34.34 litres
At rest: untrained person	70 ml × 72 = 5.04 litres
At rest: trained person	84 ml × 60 = 5.04 litres

Cardiovascular drift is the increase in heart rate that occurs due to viscous blood during prolonged endurance exercise, despite the intensity of the exercise remaining the same. This is often caused by fluid loss (sweat) and increased core body temperature, which is why it is important to maintain high fluid consumption before and during exercise.

Hormonal, neural and chemical regulation responses

There are many hormonal, neural and chemical regulation responses during physical activity:

- **anticipatory rise** — the increase in heart rate that typically occurs just before activity is to be undertaken as a result of a release of adrenaline
- **redistribution of blood** — the vascular shunt mechanism, which results in vasoconstriction (narrowing of blood vessels) and vasodilation (opening of blood vessels) to regulate blood flow
- **cardiac conduction** — relating to the electrical impulse that passes through the heart, leading to a contraction. This makes use of a group of specialised cardiac muscle cells in the walls of the heart which send signals causing it to contract
- **carbon dioxide** — exhaled as part of the breathing process
- **sympathetic system** — the part of the autonomic nervous system that speeds up heart rate
- **parasympathetic system** — the part of the autonomic nervous system that decreases heart rate

Receptors involved in the regulation of responses

Receptors involved in the regulation of responses during physical activity are located in the neural control system, which controls the use of the sympathetic and parasympathetic systems.

> **Exam tip**
>
> The cardiovascular system works in conjunction with the respiratory system (and is known as the cardio-respiratory system). An efficient system has a positive effect on the health and fitness of the individual, which is therefore a positive impact.

> **Synoptic link**
>
> It is important to remember that the hormonal, neural and chemical regulation of responses during physical activity and sport are linked to the respiratory system (page 8), which is the next topic covered.

The main receptors are:

- **chemoreceptors** — tiny structures in the carotid arteries and aortic arch that detect changes in blood acidity, caused by an increase or decrease in the concentration of carbon dioxide (Figure 1)
- **proprioceptors** — sensory nerve endings in the muscles, tendons and joints that detect changes in muscle movement
- **baroreceptors** — sensors in tissues in the aortic arch, carotid sinus, heart and pulmonary vessels that respond to changes in blood pressure to either increase or decrease heart rate

Synoptic links

This topic links closely to the neuromuscular system (page 12).

The three receptors here are also examined on page 11 when considering the regulation of pulmonary ventilation.

```
Increased levels of carbon dioxide detected
by chemoreceptors
        ↓
Increase in sympathetic nervous function
        ↓
Increase in heart rate to increase oxygen
supply to the working muscles
```

Figure 1 How chemoreceptors affect heart rate during exercise

Exam tip

Chemoreceptors, proprioceptors and baroreceptors effectively provide the 'link' between the nervous system and the cardio-respiratory system. You should also note the link between the receptors and the sympathetic and parasympathetic systems.

Transportation of oxygen

The transportation of oxygen is the primary function of blood, with the heart acting as a pump to distribute it around the body. You need to know the terms in Table 2.

Table 2

Term	Description
Haemoglobin	An iron-containing pigment found in red blood cells, which combines with oxygen to form oxyhaemoglobin.
Myoglobin	An iron-containing muscle pigment in slow-twitch muscle fibres which has a higher affinity for oxygen than haemoglobin. It stores the oxygen in the muscle fibres, which can be used quickly when exercise begins.
Oxyhaemoglobin dissociation curve (Figure 2)	This represents the relationship between oxygen and haemoglobin and how haemoglobin in the blood transports and releases oxygen.
Bohr shift	A shift to the right of the oxyhaemoglobin dissociation curve, i.e. the period when muscles require more oxygen, so the dissociation of oxygen from haemoglobin occurs more readily.
Venous return	The return of blood to the right side of the heart via the vena cava. Active mechanisms are needed to help venous return, including the skeletal muscle pump (Figure 3), the respiratory pump and pocket valves, which prevent blood flowing backwards.
Starling's law	The more blood that is pumped into the heart, the more blood must be pumped out of it, resulting in stroke volume increasing.
Arterio-venous oxygen difference (A-VO$_2$ diff)	The difference between the oxygen content of the arterial blood arriving at the muscles and the venous blood leaving the muscles. These values will vary between trained and untrained individuals as well as the intensity of an exercise session. The body does adapt (become more efficient) over time — a positive training effect.

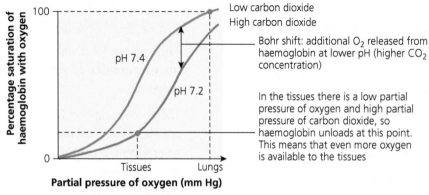

Figure 2 The oxyhaemoglobin dissociation curve

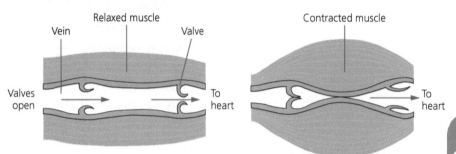

Figure 3 The skeletal muscle pump

Remember that the redistribution of blood is different at rest compared to during exercise as the skeletal muscles require more oxygen, so more blood needs to be directed to them.

> ## Exam tip
>
> Knowledge and understanding of the structure of the heart is beneficial in being able to answer questions relating to this topic.

> ## Do you know?
>
> 1 What is blood pressure?
> 2 What does adrenaline do prior to exercise?
> 3 How do chemoreceptors affect heart rate during exercise?
> 4 Describe Starling's law.
> 5 What is meant by the term 'arterio-venous oxygen difference'?

1.2 Respiratory system

You need to know

- lung volumes and the impact of these on physical activity and sport
- gas exchange systems at alveoli and muscles
- hormonal, neural and chemical regulation of pulmonary ventilation during physical activity and sport
- receptors involved in the regulation of pulmonary ventilation during physical activity
- impact of poor lifestyle choices on the respiratory system

The combined process of **inspiration** and **expiration** is known as the **mechanics of breathing**, where inspiration is the act of breathing air into the lungs and expiration is breathing air out.

Lung volumes

The different lung values (lung volumes) can be accurately monitored by using a spirometer to measure the volume of air that is inspired and expired by the lungs (see Figure 4 and Table 3).

Exam tip

Remember that the respiratory system works in conjunction with the cardiovascular system. A thorough knowledge and understanding of the structure of the lungs and the mechanics of breathing is also essential to be able to answer questions relating to this topic.

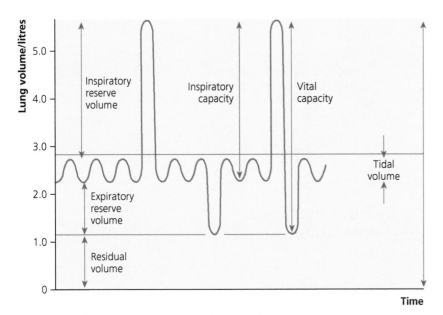

Figure 4 Spirometer trace of respiratory air

Table 3 The different parts of an individual's total lung volume and the changes that take place in these volumes during exercise

Lung volume or capacity	Definition	Change during exercise
Tidal volume	Volume of air breathed in or out per breath	Increase
Inspiratory reserve volume (IRV)	Volume of air that can be forcibly inspired after a normal breath	Decrease
Expiratory reserve volume (ERV)	Volume of air that can be forcibly expired after a normal breath	Slight decrease
Residual volume	Volume of air that remains in the lungs after maximum expiration	Remains the same
Minute ventilation	Volume of air breathed in or out per minute	Substantial increase

Gas exchange systems

Oxygen is breathed in (inspired) so that it can be diffused into the blood and transported to the cells of the body. Carbon dioxide is collected from those cells by the blood and breathed out (expired) to remove it from the body.

The process of breathing and diffusion is largely controlled by **partial pressure**. Partial pressure is the pressure exerted by an individual gas when it exists within a mixture of gases. Gas naturally moves from a high partial pressure to a low partial pressure.

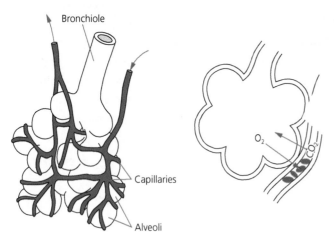

Figure 5 Diffusion in the alveoli of the lungs

In Figure 5, oxygen diffuses from an area of high partial pressure (the lungs) to an area of low partial pressure (the capillaries), while carbon dioxide moves in the opposite direction.

The principles of diffusion and partial pressure are vital to gas exchange.

Hormonal, neural and chemical regulation

There are three factors involved in the regulation of pulmonary ventilation during exercise.

Hormonal

Adrenaline is a natural stimulant made in the adrenal gland of the kidneys. It is transported to the blood and affects the nervous system by increasing breathing rate in preparation for exercise.

Neural and chemical

Neural control involves the brain and the nervous system. When chemical changes are experienced in the blood, the chemoreceptors inform the medulla in the brain. The role of chemoreceptors and the parasympathetic and sympathetic nervous systems were covered in relation to the cardiovascular system on page 7. When breathing rate needs to increase, the respiratory control centre in the brain causes this to happen.

Receptors involved in the regulation of pulmonary ventilation

- chemoreceptors
- proprioceptors
- baroreceptors

These three receptors also play a part in control of breathing rate, in conjunction with other factors such as stretch receptors (Figure 6).

Synoptic link

There is a clear link between the role of receptors in control of breathing (respiratory system) and control of heart rate (cardiovascular system).

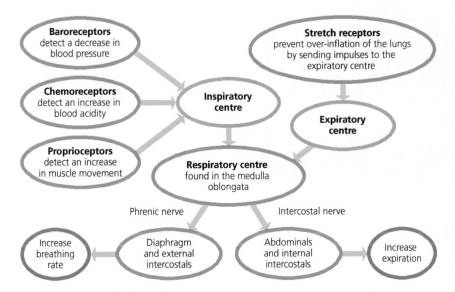

Figure 6 **Control of ventilation**

Impact of poor lifestyle choices

Smoking has a damaging effect on the respiratory system. It reduces lung function and increases breathlessness, caused by the swelling and narrowing of the airways. The whole respiratory system (and therefore the mechanics of breathing) can be adversely affected by smoking.

Remember that lifestyle is a choice. If a person chooses to smoke or to follow a sedentary lifestyle, they face the potential to suffer from breathlessness and/or breathing difficulties.

Key terms

Lifestyle How you choose to live your life

Breathlessness A feeling of being unable to breathe, sometimes caused by smoking

Exam tip

Choosing to smoke is the most damaging lifestyle choice affecting the respiratory system. There are significant negative impacts on an individual's capacity to be involved in physical activity and sport.

1.3 Neuromuscular system

You need to know

- characteristics and functions of different muscle fibre types for a variety of sporting activities, including slow twitch (type I), fast oxidative glycolytic (type IIa) and fast glycolytic (type IIx)
- role of proprioceptors in PNF
- recruitment of muscle fibres

Muscle fibre types

Each fibre type is designed for a different purpose (see Table 4).

Table 4 **Some characteristics of slow and fast twitch muscle fibres**

Characteristic	Type I	Type IIa	Type IIx
Contraction speed (ms^{-1})	Slow (110)	Fast (50)	Fast (50)
Motor neurone conduction capacity	Slow	Fast	Fast
Force produced	Low	High	High
Fatigability	Low	Medium	High
Mitochondrial density	High	Medium	Low
Myoglobin content	High	Medium	Low
Capillary density	High	Medium	Low
Aerobic capacity	Very high	Medium	Low
Anaerobic capacity	Low	High	Very high

Thus the varying fibre types have particular uses in sport:

- **slow twitch fibres** are particularly useful for long-distance endurance events, e.g. a marathon
- **fast twitch type IIa** are particularly useful for activities of a medium to high intensity, e.g. an 800-metre run
- **fast twitch type IIx** are particularly useful for explosive, fast events, e.g. sprinting, discus throw, javelin

Synoptic link

Muscle fibre types relate to energy systems in that slow twitch fibres do more work aerobically, whereas type IIx do more work anaerobically.

Training can have an effect on fibre types. Although the size of muscle fibres is genetically determined, it is possible to increase size through training, resulting in hypertrophy.

The role of proprioceptors in PNF

Proprioceptive neuromuscular facilitation (PNF) is an advanced stretching technique which makes use of **CRAC** (contract – relax – antagonist – relax).

Muscle spindles

These are sensitive proprioceptors that lie between skeletal muscle fibres. They detect how far and how fast a muscle is being stretched. During PNF stretching, the spindles detect the stretch and trigger a stretch reflex, preventing overstretching.

Golgi tendon organs

These are located between the muscle fibre and tendon and they detect the level of tension in a muscle. Autogenic inhibition is when the golgi tendon organs sense the muscle tension and send inhibitory signals to the medulla, which allows the antagonist muscle to lengthen and relax.

Exam tip

Muscle stretching is important both pre- and post-exercise so you should be aware of the types of stretching which are most suitable and appropriate, as well as the role and importance of muscle spindles and the golgi tendon organs during stretching.

The recruitment of muscle fibres

The interaction of all the factors below enables effective muscular contractions to take place and thus allows sporting actions to occur. Therefore, it is important to be aware of the specific role that each one performs:

- **motor unit:** this consists of a motor neurone and its muscle fibres. Only one type of muscle fibre can be found in a particular motor unit, so each muscle is made up of many motor units which vary in size
- **spatial summation:** this is when the strength of a contraction changes by rotating the frequency of the impulse to motor units to delay fatigue

Key terms

Hypertrophy Where the muscle has become bigger and stronger

Aerobic With oxygen; for low to medium intensity exercise where the oxygen demands of the muscles can be met

Anaerobic Without oxygen; for high intensity exercise where the oxygen demand of muscles is so high that it cannot be met

Stretch reflex The reflex action that causes the muscle to contract to prevent overstretching and therefore reduce the risk of injury

Tendon A cord or band of dense, tough, inelastic, white, fibrous tissue which connects muscle with bone

Synoptic link

PNF stretching can be linked to flexibility training (active, passive, static and ballistic) when used as a method of injury prevention, rehabilitation and recovery.

Key term

Motor neurone Nerve cells which transmit the brain's instructions as electrical impulses to the muscles

- **wave summation:** this when the nerve impulse is repeated with no time to relax, resulting in a smooth, sustained contraction
- **tetanic contraction:** this is a forceful, sustained, smooth muscle contraction caused by a series of fast repeating stimuli
- **the 'all or none law':** once a motor neurone stimulates the muscle fibres, either all of them contract or none of them do. This is because it is impossible for a motor unit to only partially contract

Do you know?

1 What are the characteristics of a slow twitch type I fibre?
2 What activities are fast twitch type IIx fibres suited to?
3 What is a muscle spindle apparatus?
4 What is meant by the term 'wave summation'?

1.4 Musculo-skeletal system and analysis of movement

You need to know

- joint actions in the sagittal plane/transverse axis
- joint actions in the frontal plane/sagittal axis
- joint actions in the transverse plane/longitudinal axis
- types of joint, articulating bones, main agonists and antagonists, types of muscle contraction

The muscular system and skeletal system combine to form the musculo-skeletal system, and this is what enables movement to take place. It is important to know the main skeletal bones and muscles of the body as well as being familiar with the various forms of connective tissue and joints which allow any movement to take place.

Joint actions

When performing any activity, a body or body parts will move in one of the following planes or even in all three of them (Figure 7). You should be aware of a range of basic movements or actions and the planes and axes of movement which are enabling that specific sporting movement or action to take place.

Synoptic link

Planes and axes of movement can relate to transfer of learning. Movement in the same plane and around the same axis may be easier to positively transfer.

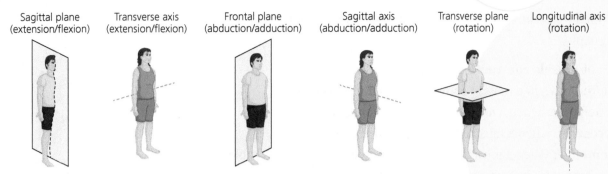

Figure 7 Planes and axes of movement

Sagittal plane/transverse axis

The sagittal plane divides the body into right and left halves. The transverse axis runs from side to side across the body. Movements in these areas include:

- movements at the shoulder and hip (both ball and socket joints), which consist of flexion, extension and hyperextension
- movements at the elbow and knee (hinge/synovial joints), which consist of flexion and extension
- movements at the ankle, which consist of plantar flexion and dorsiflexion

Frontal plane/sagittal axis

The frontal plane divides the body into front and back, while the sagittal axis runs from front to back. Movements in these areas occur at the shoulder and the hip (both ball and socket joints), which consist of adduction and abduction.

Transverse plane/longitudinal axis

The transverse plane divides the body into upper and lower halves, while the longitudinal axis runs from top to bottom. Movements in these areas also occur at the shoulder and the hip (both ball and socket joints) which consist of **horizontal** abduction and adduction.

Types of joints

A **joint** is the point at which two or more bones meet. There are three types of joint:

- fibrous or 'fixed'
- cartilaginous or 'slightly moveable'
- synovial or 'freely moveable'

Articulating bones are the bones that meet and move at the joint.

Main agonists and antagonists are the pairs of muscles that allow movement to occur. Muscles cannot push, they only pull, so the

Key terms

Flexion Decreasing the angle between the bones of a joint

Extension Increasing the angle between the bones at a joint

Hyperextension Increasing the angle beyond 180 degrees between the bones of a joints

Adduction Movement of a limb towards the midline of the body

Abduction Movement of a limb away from the midline of the body

Exam tip

You should have studied two types of synovial joints — the ball and socket joint and the hinge joint. Examples include the hip, shoulder, elbow, knee and ankle.

Key terms

Agonist The muscle that is responsible for the movement that is occurring

Antagonist The muscle that works in opposition to the agonist to help produce a coordinated movement

combined (opposing) actions of the agonists and antagonists create movement.

Types of **muscle contraction** include:

- **isotonic:** when a muscle contracts to create movement
- **concentric:** when a muscle shortens under tension
- **eccentric:** when a muscle lengthens under tension
- **isometric:** when a muscle is under tension but there is no visible movement (as it does not actually lengthen or shorten)

Do you know?

1 Movement in the sagittal plane always corresponds to movement around which axis?

2 Movement in the transverse plane always corresponds to movement around which axis?

3 Movement in the frontal plane always corresponds to movement around which axis?

4 What is an agonist muscle?

5 What does the term 'isometric' mean?

1.5 Energy systems

You need to know

- energy transfer in the body
- energy continuum of physical activity
- energy transfer during short duration/high intensity exercise
- energy transfer during long duration/lower intensity exercise
- factors affecting VO_2 max/aerobic power
- measurements of energy expenditure
- impact of specialist training methods on energy systems
- the three phases in which energy systems are important: prior to exercise, during exercise of differing intensities and during recovery

Exam tip

It is important that you have a good, basic overview of each energy system and that you can link them to activities/sports in which they are used.

Energy transfer in the body

Energy is needed by the body at all times but as we exercise, more energy is required.

The aerobic energy system

When exercise intensity levels are low and the oxygen supply is high then the aerobic (with oxygen) energy system is the preferred energy pathway (Figure 8). The aerobic system has three stages:

- glycolysis
- the Krebs cycle (or citric acid cycle)
- the electron transport chain

Beta oxidation is when fatty acids are converted into acetyl co-enzyme A, which is the entry molecule for the Krebs cycle.

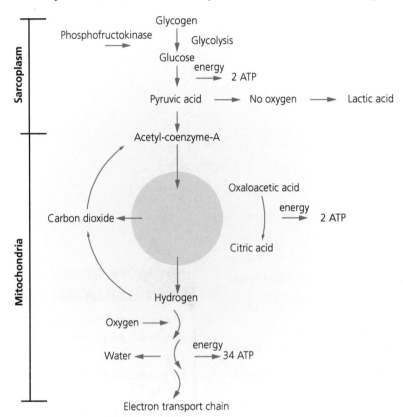

Figure 8 **Summary of the aerobic system**

The anaerobic ATP–PC energy system

The anaerobic (without oxygen) energy system is preferred when exercise levels are required for a short maximal movement (such as sprinting or long jump take off) and ATP (adenosine triphosphate) and PC (phosphocreatine) are the energy systems used. It can last for up to 10 seconds.

The equation for this system is:

phosphocreatine (PC) → phosphate (Pi) + creatine (C) + energy

The energy is then used to resynthesize ATP:

energy + ADP + Pi → ATP

Anaerobic glycolytic system

This is an intermediate anaerobic system, which can supply energy for a short time (up to 3 minutes) for high intensity activity. This system is also referred to as the short-term lactate anaerobic system (Figure 9).

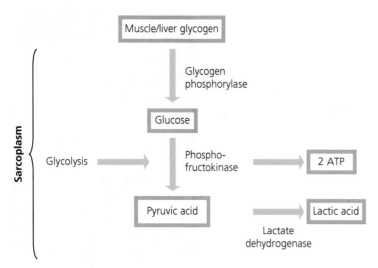

Figure 9 **The lactate anaerobic system**

Energy continuum of physical activity

An **energy continuum** is required by all physical activity and sport of different intensities and durations.

The demand for energy rises rapidly when exercise starts. The energy continuum regulates which energy system is used and which will be the predominant provider. The intensity and duration of the activity are the main factors determining this (Figure 10).

The differences in ATP generation between fast and slow twitch muscle fibres also determine which energy system is used:
■ as slow twitch fibres are used for low to medium intensity activity, aerobic respiration will be the main energy source
■ fast twitch fibres are used for high intensity activities, so anaerobic energy systems will be the main energy source

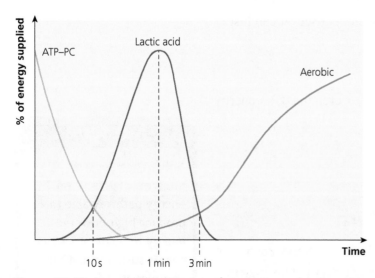

Figure 10 **The energy continuum related to exercise duration**

Energy transfer

Short duration/high intensity exercise

For short-duration, high intensity activity, the energy systems in use will be anaerobic, i.e. the ATP–PC/anaerobic glycolytic system. In the short-term lactate anaerobic system:

■ energy has to be produced rapidly and this results in lactate accumulation in the muscles

■ this slows down enzyme activity, which in turn affects the breakdown of glycogen, causing muscle fatigue

■ as the exercise intensity increases, the body moves from working aerobically to anaerobically as the lactate threshold is reached

■ lactate levels will continue to increase as the OBLA point is reached

Sprint/power performers have a much better anaerobic endurance level than non-elite performers, as their bodies have adapted through training to allow them to cope with higher levels of lactate. Overall, this means that they are able to work at higher intensities for longer before fatigue sets in.

Long duration/lower intensity exercise

For this type of activity, the energy system in use will be aerobic.

Oxygen consumption during exercise

During exercise, the body uses oxygen to produce energy. Oxygen consumption is the amount of oxygen we need to produce ATP, which is usually referred to as VO_2. As soon as exercise is underway, more oxygen is needed and used to provide more ATP, so oxygen consumption increases. Both maximal and submaximal oxygen deficit occur as a direct result of this.

Oxygen consumption during recovery

■ recovery involves the body returning to its pre-exercise state

■ as any physical activity finishes, oxygen consumption is still high (more than it was at rest) as the performer is taking in extra oxygen in order to recover

■ this is why performers often experience breathlessness when they stop an activity (EPOC)

Key terms

Lactate This is not the same as lactic acid. Lactic acid breaks down, releasing hydrogen ions (H+), the remaining compound then combines with sodium ions (Na+) or potassium ions (K+) to form the salt lactate. This then accumulates in the muscles, slowing down enzyme activity and causing muscle fatigue

Lactate accumulation Where lactate levels increase as a by-product of increased exercise intensity

Fatigue Either physical or mental, fatigue is a feeling of extreme or severe tiredness due to a build-up of lactic acid or working for long periods of time

Lactate threshold The point during exercise at which lactic acid quickly accumulates in the blood

OBLA (onset blood lactate accumulation) The point at which blood lactate levels go above 4 millimoles per litre

Submaximal oxygen deficit When there is not enough oxygen available at the start of exercise to provide all the energy (ATP) aerobically

Maximal oxygen deficit (also known as maximal accumulated oxygen deficit or MAOD) When the performer lacks oxygen at the start of exercise and they have to work more anaerobically

Factors affecting VO₂ max

An individual's VO_2 max (or aerobic power) is the maximum volume of oxygen that can be consumed by their muscles in one minute. This will determine their endurance levels. Specific endurance based training can increase a person's VO_2 max, as the body adapts to be able to take up more oxygen. See Table 5.

> **Key term**
>
> **EPOC** (excess post-exercise oxygen consumption) The restoration of oxygen consumed during recovery which would have been consumed at rest during the same time

Table 5 Factors affecting VO₂ max

Physiological	<ul><li>increased maximum cardiac output</li><li>increased stroke volume/ejection fraction/cardiac hypertrophy</li><li>greater heart rate range</li><li>less oxygen being used for heart muscle so more available to muscles</li><li>increased levels of haemoglobin and red blood cell count</li><li>increased stores of glycogen and triglycerides</li><li>increased myoglobin content</li><li>increased capillarisation around the muscles</li><li>increased number and size of mitochondria</li><li>increased surface area of alveoli</li><li>increased lactate tolerance</li></ul>
Training	VO_2 max can be improved by up to 10–20% following aerobic training (continuous, fartlek and aerobic interval).
Lifestyle	Smoking, sedentary lifestyle, poor diet and poor fitness can all reduce VO_2 max values.
Body composition	A higher percentage of body fat decreases VO_2 max.
Gender	Men generally have approx. 20% higher VO_2 max than women.
Age	As we get older, our VO_2 max declines as our body systems become less efficient.
Genetics	Inherited factors of physiology limit possible improvement.

Measurements of energy expenditure

Being able to measure how much energy needs to be expended is vital for performers to be able to identify their level of fitness and also plan their training accordingly.

- **indirect calorimetry:** this measures how much carbon dioxide is produced and how much oxygen is consumed during the gaseous exchange process at rest and during aerobic exercise. Using this method, VO_2 and VO_2 max can be measured accurately
- **lactate sampling:** a small blood sample is taken from a performer to check blood lactate levels, used as a means of measuring exercise intensity. This method also gives an indication of level of fitness and can be used to inform a training regime
- **VO₂ max test:** there are several tests which can be used to measure this, including the 'bleep test' (progressive shuttle run) and accurate tests that can be performed in sports laboratories

> **Key term**
>
> **Calorimetry** The calculation of heat in physical changes and chemical reactions

■ **respiratory exchange ratio (RER):** this is the ratio of carbon dioxide produced compared to oxygen consumed, used as another measure of exercise intensity

Specialist training methods

The following training methods will impact on energy systems to make performers more effective.

Altitude training

This is usually carried out at 2000 m or more above sea level as the partial pressure of oxygen is lower here (effectively there is less oxygen), so the body adapts by creating more red blood cells to carry oxygen. The additional oxygen-carrying blood cell is an advantage for endurance athletes/performers returning to sea level to compete. This is not a permanent change and is only a short-term advantage.

High intensity interval training (HIIT)

This is an exercise strategy which alternates periods of short, high intensity exercise with less intense recovery periods. Four main variables are involved:

■ the duration of the work phase
■ the intensity or speed of the work phase
■ the duration of the recovery phase
■ the number of work phases and recovery phases

Plyometrics

This is training using plyometric exercises such as bounding or depth jumping. It is designed to increase power by using an eccentric contraction followed by a larger concentric contraction.

Speed, agility, quickness (SAQ)

Speed, agility, quickness (SAQ) training combines speed, agility and quickness. There are many variations and forms of this training and it is relatively easy to plan an SAQ session to make it sport-specific.

> ## Exam tip
>
> The best way for you to know and understand these terms is to measure your own levels in the four categories and take the tests.

> ## Key terms
>
> **Eccentric contraction** Where the tension in the muscle increases as it lengthens
>
> **Concentric contraction** Where the tension in the muscle increases as it shortens
>
> **Speed** The ability to move the body in one direction as fast as possible
>
> **Agility** The ability to accelerate, decelerate, stabilise and quickly change directions with proper posture
>
> **Quickness** The ability to react and change body position with a maximum rate of force production

> ## Exam tip
>
> Just as, you can measure your energy expenditure you can also (with the exception of altitude training) experience these training methods to gain a better understanding of each.

Do you know?

1 Which energy system would be used for short, intense exercise?
2 Which energy system would be used for high intensity exercise of up to 3 minutes?
3 The Krebs cycle is part of which energy system?
4 What does EPOC stand for?
5 Describe SAQ training.

End of section 1 questions

1 What impact can physical activity have on health and fitness?
2 What is the process of gas exchange and what role does it play in the mechanics of breathing?
3 What are the three different muscle twitch fibres and why are their differences important when considering the energy continuum?
4 What are the main planes and axes of movement?
5 Differentiate between aerobic and anaerobic energy systems.
6 What are the different ways of measuring energy expenditure?

2 Skill acquisition

2.1 Characteristics of skill

You need to know
- characteristics of skill
- use of skill continua
- justification of placement on skill continua
- transfer of learning
- how transfer of learning impacts on skill development

Skill is defined as the learned ability to bring about predetermined results with the minimum outlay of time, energy or both.

In more detail:
- all skills are learned. Natural ability may help a performer but skills need to be developed
- skills are controlled and accurate. They are carried out in a controlled manner to gain an accurate result
- skill needs to be consistent. The performer is deemed to be 'skilled' if they can reproduce that skill with the same success regularly
- the skill is aesthetically pleasing, i.e. it must look good. In some activities (e.g. gymnastics) marks are allocated for this
- skills also need to be fluent, economical, smooth and efficient. At the highest level, skilled performance looks effortless

When you are considering skill acquisition, it is important to remember that this includes developing new skills as well as optimising the development of existing skills.

Key term

Efficient Performing a skill effectively with the minimum outlay of effort

Table 6 **Definitions of skill continua**

Skill continuum	Definition	Example
Open–closed	Open skills are performed in a certain way to deal with a changing or unstable environment. This generally involves people who affect how the skill is carried out.	Passing the ball in football
	Closed skills are not affected by the environment or performers within it. They are essentially carried out the way same each time.	Shot put throw
Discrete–serial–continuous	A discrete skill has a clear beginning and end.	Tennis serve
	A serial skill contains several discrete skills in order to make a more integrated movement.	Triple jump
	A continuous skill has no clear beginning and end and often the end of one part or subroutine of the skill is the start of the next part.	Cycling

Skill continuum	Definition	Example
Gross–fine	A gross movement (required for a gross skill) is where you use large muscle groups to perform big, strong, powerful movements.	Sprinting
	A fine movement (required for fine skills) is a small and precise movement, showing high levels of accuracy and coordination, and it involves the use of a small set of muscles.	Golf put
Self-paced–externally paced	A self-paced skill is one which begins when the performer decides to start it.	Penalty kick
	An externally paced skill is one where the skill is started by an external factor.	Sprint start
High–low organisation	A high-organisation skill is a highly organised skill, which is not easily broken down into parts, often because it is quickly done and the parts of the skill merge into one.	Badminton smash
	A low-organisation skill is easily broken down into parts or subroutines.	Swimming stroke
Simple–complex	A simple skill is a basic skill with few decisions to be processed.	Forward roll
	A complex skill is far more difficult with many decisions to be processed.	Dribbling a hockey ball

Use of skill continua

Skills need to be practised in order for a performer to improve. Using skill continua (Table 6) can help to ensure that the correct form of practice can be selected and used.

Skills are classified depending on whether they meet the criteria for each aspect of continua, although you can argue a classification of your choice with a suitable justification.

Skill continua types and examples

The placement of a skill on each of the continua can change depending on the situation. If a skill is practised in isolation, when the performer is on their own, this can be very different from a team game situation, with team-mates and opposition present.

For example, a basketball dribble on your own would be a closed skill, whereas against opposition, it becomes an open skill.

Badminton serving could be classified as self-paced as the server decides when to serve. However, it is also classified as open, as the serve is affected by the position of the opponent.

Exam tip

Some of the main characteristics of skill can be remembered by using the acronym 'RACE FACE':
Result achieves desired goal
Aesthetically pleasing
Controlled
Efficient
Fluent
Accurate
Consistent
Economical

Synoptic link

It is possible that the effective production of a skill is affected by the composition of the fast twitch fibres a performer has. For example, without a high percentage of fast twitch type IIx fibres, a performer may struggle to react quickly enough to catch a cricket ball.

Transfer of learning

Transfer of learning refers to how learned sporting skills can be transferred from one sport to another. Sometimes this transfer works well. Sometimes the transfer of this learning has little effect, no effect or even a negative effect.

It can be possible for skills to be used in more than one activity, e.g. fielding skills in cricket would be equally used in rounders.

Different types of transfer

Positive transfer

This is when the learning of one skill helps the learning of another.

For example, a tennis serve **positively transfers** to a volleyball serve. This is because the action of throwing up and hitting through is very similar.

Negative transfer

This is when the action of one skill hinders the learning of another.

For example, a tennis forehand **negatively transfers** to a badminton underarm clear. This is because a tennis forehand involves a relatively straight arm and fixed wrist, whereas the badminton clear involves a whipping action created by the flicked wrist movement.

Zero transfer

This is when the learning of one skill has no effect on another as the two skills have no similarities. For example, a golf swing has **zero transfer** to a pass in basketball.

Bilateral transfer

This is when the learning of one skill is transferred across the body from limb to limb.

For example, passing with the right foot in football has **bilateral transfer** to passing with the left foot in football.

Ensuring positive impact

Clearly, positive transfer is the primary positive effect which any performer or coach should be aiming for, so it is important to ensure that training is realistic and relevant.

For example, the skill of catching a netball can be positively transferred to catching a basketball.

Do you know?

1 Define what is meant by the term 'skill'.
2 Name four characteristics of skilled performance.
3 Define what is meant by a 'gross' skill.
4 Define what is meant by a 'fine' skill.
5 Is a sprint start a self-paced or externally paced skill?

2.2 Impact of skill classification on structure of practice for learning

You need to know

- methods of presenting practice
- types of practice
- how knowledge of skill classification informs practice structure (presentation and type) to allow learning/ development of skills

Having classified a skill, the next choice is how to practise the skill.

For example, a closed skill could be done on your own in your own time, whereas an open skill would require a changing environment. Thus, how to present the practice is key to ensuring success.

Methods of presenting practice

Table 7

Skill	Definition	Example	Advantages	Disadvantages
Whole	Practising the skill in its entirety, not breaking it down into subroutines.	Golf swing.	Helps to create a whole motor programme for the skill. Good for simple skills.	Could be tiring completing the whole skill or unrealistic for the performer to complete the whole skill.
Progressive part	Practising the first part of the skill and then the rest of the parts are added gradually.	Dance routine.	Realistic to add sections on when the participant is ready. Builds confidence. Useful for cognitive performers.	Time-consuming. Difficult to create links between the parts.
Whole–part–whole	The whole skill is attempted, then each separate part of the task is practised (either individually or after specific weaknesses are highlighted) and then put back into the whole skill, which is repeated again.	Experienced tennis player having a problem with their serve.	Targets specific parts with weaknesses which can help to motivate the performer.	Sometimes lose the relevance of the part being practised to the whole.

Exam tip

You are likely to be asked questions regarding the advantages and disadvantages of the three practice methods described above. Try to link your knowledge of the stages of learning on page 29 to the ways of presenting practice. For example, an autonomous person performing a relatively simple skill would use whole practice.

Synoptic link

A link can be made from this topic to energy systems. A performer can only complete a whole practice if they can do so without getting too tired.

Types of practice

Table 8

Skill	Definition	Advantages	Disadvantages
Massed	Continuous, so there are no rest intervals between sessions. These are often used when there are unlikely to be any changes needed to the skill, so numerous repetitions of it are feasible.	Good for fit, motivated, autonomous performers enacting relatively simple skills.	Requires suitable fitness and motivation. Can become monotonous.
Distributed	There are rest intervals between sessions. This is often used when practising open skills, due to their unpredictable nature, so the performer may need a break to reassess, regroup, consider changes or additions.	Good for beginners to allow rest, mental rehearsal and to gain feedback.	Can be time-consuming.

Skill	Definition	Advantages	Disadvantages
Variable	Drills and types of practice are changed/varied so that the performers learn to adapt to changes in the environment.	Provides variety and can motivate performers. Helps to develop schema.	Can be time-consuming and confuse performers as to what their goal actually is.
Mental	The performer goes through the movement in their mind without any physical movement. This often occurs just before a major event or between periods of physical practice.	Builds confidence. Lowers anxiety. Performer feels 'prepared'.	Performers may overthink and start to doubt themselves.

Do you know?

1 What is meant by 'massed practice'?
2 Would a beginner tend to need massed or distributed practice?

Exam tip

You are likely to be asked questions regarding the advantages and disadvantages of the three types of practice described above. You are also likely to be asked how methods and types of practice can be combined most effectively.

Synoptic link

The type of practice to be selected can link to many topics, such as skill classification and self-efficacy and Vealey's model of self-confidence. If a performer feels confident while practising, they are more likely to persist.

2.3 Principles and theories of learning and performance

You need to know

- stages of learning and how feedback differs between the different stages of learning (cognitive, associative and autonomous)
- learning plateaus (their causes and solutions)
- cognitive theories — insight learning (Gestalt)
- behaviourism — operant conditioning (Skinner)
- social learning — observational learning (Bandura)
- constructivism — social development theory (Vygotsky)
- how theories of learning impact on skill development

Stages of learning

There are three distinctive stages of learning through which a performer transitions, from beginner to expert (Figure 11).

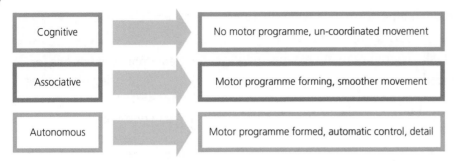

Figure 11 The stages of learning and development of motor programmes

Cognitive

- the first stage of learning (beginner)
- understanding and subroutines are explored by trial and error
- the performer has to consider their actions carefully and tends to rely on help and guidance from others
- for example, a beginner at tennis

Associative

- the second stage of learning
- as **motor programmes** develop, performance becomes smoother
- this is an interim stage as the performer moves from being a competent beginner to an accomplished performer
- for example, a recreational golfer

Autonomous

- the final stage of learning
- experienced by an expert when movement is detailed and specific
- motor programmes are fully developed and can help in the fine control of the action
- for example, a professional athlete

Key term

Motor programmes The stored commands which enable the production of a desired movement

Learning plateau

Learning and success rates can be drawn in a graph to show the rate of improvement or deterioration (Figure 12).

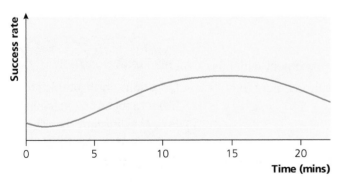

Figure 12 A typical learning curve showing the rate of improvement when attempting a closed skill over a 20-minute period

A learning plateau is the period during performance when there are no signs of improvement and the performer does not seem to be getting any better at doing the task. There are many reasons why such a plateau may be experienced:

- lack of motivation
- boredom
- poor coaching/ guidance
- limited ability
- target setting too low
- fatigue
- drive reduction
- poor fitness

There are many methods that can be used to overcome and/or prevent the plateau from occurring:

- changing targets or tasks
- changing coaches
- resting to combat fatigue
- more variety to avoid boredom
- better quality feedback and guidance

Plateauing may occur more than once. A plateau may occur at various points when taking part in an activity, as the skills become more complex and you move through the stages of learning.

Theories of learning

You need to be aware of different theories related to how we learn.

Cognitive: insight learning (Gestalt)

Insight learning is also known as a Gestaltist approach, where the skill being learned is treated holistically (i.e. there is a 'eureka' moment).

The participant develops an understanding of the skill requirements, and the process involves perception and the interpretation of the stimuli. The participant takes into consideration aspects of the environmental display, and problem-solving and discovery/finding out also take place.

Although it can take longer to learn and is time-consuming, it is good for helping the participant to become adaptable.

Behaviourism: operant conditioning (Skinner)

This involves changing behaviour by the use of reinforcement which is given after the desired response (Figure 13). This reinforcement may be positive or negative as both strengthen the stimulus–response (SR) bond.

An example of positive reinforcement is where praise is given when the correct response is given to the stimulus.

Negative reinforcement involves the removal of an unpleasant stimulus when the correct response is given. For example, if a coach regularly criticises a performer, this criticism is simply removed when they provide the correct response.

Reinforcement
Positive
Negative
Pleasant stimulus to encourage correct response
Withdrawing unpleasant stimulus to encourage correct response

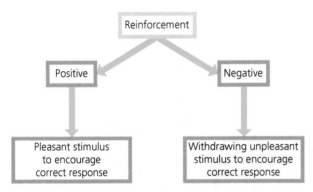

Figure 13 **How reinforcement is used as part of operant conditioning**

Punishment is occasionally used to break the stimulus–response bond, so that the performer is encouraged to develop the correct response.

Social learning theory: observational learning (Bandura)

Observational learning occurs through observing the behaviour of others and copying their behaviour in the pursuit of reinforcement (Figure 14).

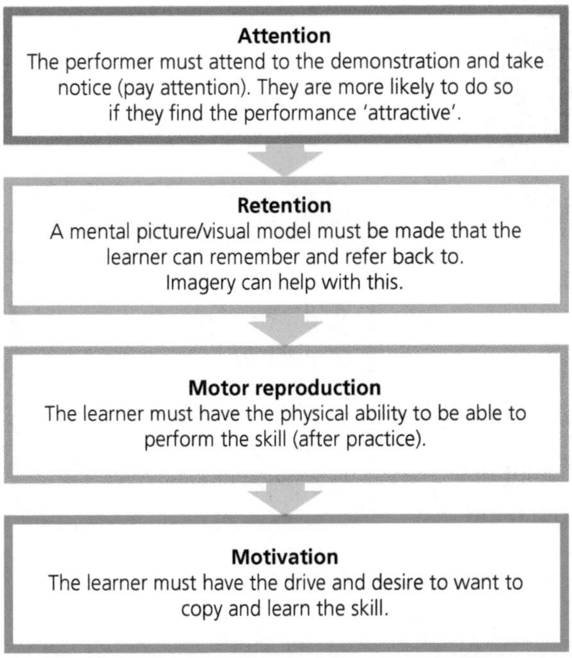

Attention
The performer must attend to the demonstration and take notice (pay attention). They are more likely to do so if they find the performance 'attractive'.
Retention
A mental picture/visual model must be made that the learner can remember and refer back to. Imagery can help with this.
Motor reproduction
The learner must have the physical ability to be able to perform the skill (after practice).
Motivation
The learner must have the drive and desire to want to copy and learn the skill.

Figure 14 **The stages of observational learning**

> **Exam tip**
>
> Remember the stages of observational learning using the acronym '**ARMM**':
> **A**ttention
> **R**etention
> **M**otor reproduction
> **M**otivation

Constructivism: social development theory (Vygotsky)

Social development theory explores how behaviour is influenced by **social interaction**. Constructivism develops this further, exploring how

> **Key terms**
>
> **Social interaction** Being with others and learning from them
>
> **Motor reproduction** Having the ability to replicate a task

skills are learned, taking into account the use of a 'zone of proximal development'. The three stages of proximal development are:

1 What can I do alone?
2 What can I do with help?
3 What can I not do yet?

For example, a performer may well feel that they can hit a hockey ball (stage one). With help, they believe they could learn to do a push pass (stage two). They know they cannot yet do a flick (stage 3).

Synoptic link

All learning theories have links to self-efficacy and Vealey's model of self-confidence. As a human learns in a suitable way, they develop self-confidence and self-efficacy in specific situations.

Do you know?

1 What are the three stages of constructivism?
2 What are the three stages of learning?
3 What is an SR bond?

2.4 Use of guidance and feedback

You need to know

- methods of guidance
- the different purposes and types of feedback
- how feedback and guidance impact on skill development

Key terms

Manual With the guidance of physical contact from a coach

Mechanical With the guidance of an aid or piece of equipment

Methods of guidance

Guidance can be provided through four different methods (see Table 9):

- **visual** — demonstration
- **verbal** — explanation
- manual — physical support
- mechanical — artificial aid

Table 9

Term	Definition	Example	Advantages	Disadvantages
Verbal	Spoken guidance. Receiving it involves using your sense of hearing.	Listening to someone giving instructions.	Helps to explain a visual image. Provides detail in relation to technique and tactics.	Can be time-consuming and may cause information overload. Language used can be difficult to understand.

Term	Definition	Example	Advantages	Disadvantages
Visual	Involves the performer being able to actually see something, using the sense of sight.	A demonstration, photograph, video or YouTube™ clip.	Good for cognitive performers. Creates a visual image as the performer can see the guidance.	Important that the demonstration is clear and correct, otherwise it is ineffective.
Manual	Where the performer could actually be assisted in a physical movement.	Supporting someone performing a gymnastic vault.	Eliminates danger and builds confidence.	Performer can become too reliant on the manual guidance. Overuse can mean the performer does not get to 'feel' what the skill is like without the guidance.
Mechanical	Involves the use of objects or aids.	The RoboGolfPro machine, used by professional golfers, physically guides the players through a perfect swing.	Good for athletes with disabilities. Eliminates danger and instils confidence.	Performer can become over-reliant on the mechanical aid and may feel they cannot perform without it.

Remember that cognitive performers may need visual guidance first, so they can make a mental picture of what the skill looks like. They may also need manual and/or mechanical guidance to build up confidence.

Purposes and types of feedback

Feedback is an essential part of learning. As feedback is received, a performer can gauge what needs to change or remain the same about their performance. There are different types of feedback:

- **knowledge of performance:** this involves receiving information about the performance itself, possibly regarding the technique used and how to improve it
- **knowledge of results:** the feedback the performer gets through the end result of their performance, or by being told by an observer at the end of the performance
- **positive and negative:** being able to tell the performer what was good and correct about the performance (positive) and what was bad or incorrect about the performance (negative)
- **intrinsic:** feedback from themselves
- **extrinsic:** feedback from others

Synoptic link

Guidance works in tandem with feedback. As guidance is used, so feedback is received.

Exam tip

Remember the types of feedback using the acronym 'NIPPER':
Negative
Intrinsic
Positive
Performance (knowledge of)
Extrinsic
Results (knowledge of)

Exam tip

Questions on this topic are likely to focus on how feedback and guidance can impact on skill development. Try to match the types of feedback and guidance to the stages of learning. For example, cognitive performers tend to cope better with extrinsic, positive feedback and knowledge of results. As they improve through the stages of learning, they can interpret intrinsic feedback and accept negative feedback and knowledge of performance.

Synoptic link

Feedback holds many links to self-efficacy and confidence. If feedback is positive, it can increase a performer's confidence.

Do you know?

1 What are the different types of feedback?
2 What is 'manual guidance'?
3 What is a possible disadvantage of using mechanical guidance?

2.5 Memory models

You need to know

- general information processing models including a basic model involving input, decision making, output and feedback
- Baddeley and Hitch's working memory model
- the efficiency of information processing, including Whiting's information processing model for a range of sporting contexts
- definitions of and the relationship between reaction time, response time and movement time
- factors affecting response time
- definitions of anticipation
- strategies to improve response time
- Schmidt's schema theory and its application to sporting situations
- strategies to improve information processing

Basic information processing model

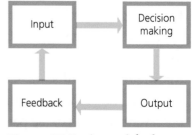

Figure 15 **Basic model of information processing**

Information processing is the action of interpreting information to make a suitable decision. The processing of this information is formed of four key stages, as shown in Figure 15.

Input

Input involves what has been received from the senses:

- sight
- hearing
- touch
- balance
- kinaesthesis

A performer makes use of selective attention, by filtering relevant information and deciding what the most important cue from the display is. In doing so, the performer makes use of receptor systems, proprioceptors and perception.

Key terms

Kinaesthesis Perception/ awareness of body position and muscular tension, informed by proprioceptors

Selective attention The process of filtering relevant from the irrelevant information

Display The sporting environment

Decision making

Decision making involves the performer making the appropriate choice or response to the selectively attended information from their memory system. This includes the **short-term memory (STM)**, which is retained for about 30 seconds, and **long-term memory (LTM)**, which stretches back over years. There is also the **working memory**, which is the **central executive** (or control system) that performs a number of functions in the three subsystems (this three-part model was first proposed by Baddeley and Hitch, see below).

Output

The output is where the information that has already been processed is sent to the muscles in order to carry out the selected response.

Feedback

Feedback can be received by the performer themselves (intrinsic feedback) and/or from others (extrinsic feedback), such a teacher or coach.

Below is an example that summarises the whole decision-making process.

When passing a netball:
1 **input:** information from the display, such as where the players are, how the ball feels, how balanced you are etc.
2 **decision making:** draws upon information from the last 30 seconds to decide to pass. If a pass has not been made in the last 30 seconds then a motor programme is retrieved from the LTM
3 **output:** the decision to pass is sent to the appropriate muscles via the effector mechanisms

Baddeley and Hitch's working memory model

This model proposes that several memory stores 'work' to allow the brain to choose a suitable response to a given situation.

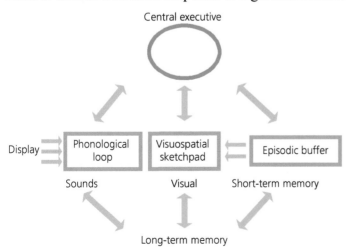

Figure 16 **The working memory model (Baddeley and Hitch)**

In Figure 16:

- the **central executive** has overall control of the information and identifies which of the subsystems should be used
- the **phonological loop** deals with sounds/auditory information and translates what these sounds mean
- the **visuospatial sketchpad** deals with what can be seen and where
- the **episodic buffer** coordinates the phonological loop and the visuospatial sketchpad, to be sent to the long-term memory to start to form a suitable motor programme
- the **long-term memory** is an infinite store of motor programmes and memories

The working model recognises the different components included within the working memory and how they work together to interpret information from the display to make a suitable decision.

The efficiency of information processing

Whiting's information-processing model

Whiting's information-processing model begins with the display and ends with feedback being received after the decision has been made (Figure 17).

> ### Synoptic link
>
> This section has important links with the neuromuscular system, musculo-skeletal system and mechanics of movement topics in Section 1.

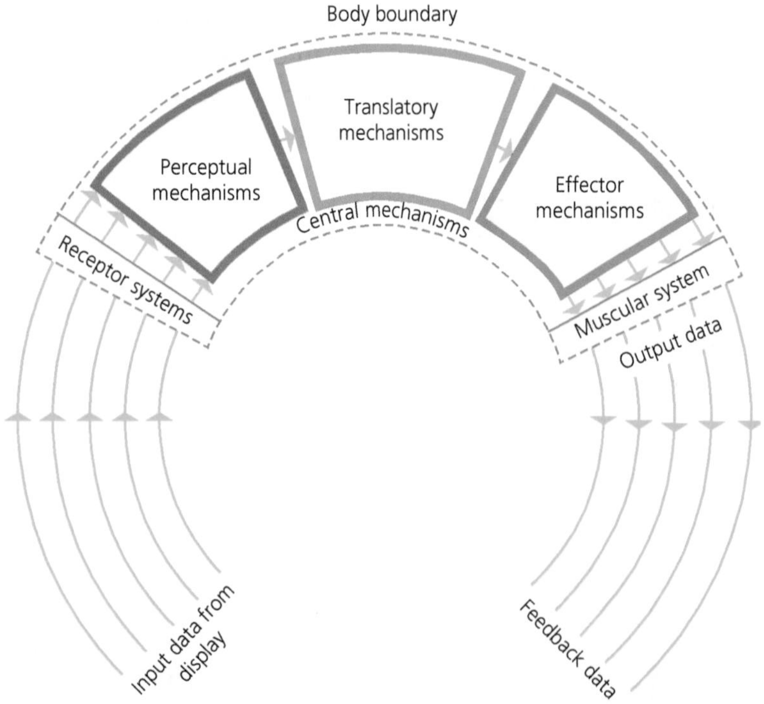

Figure 17 Whiting's information-processing model; Whiting 1969, *Acquiring Ball Skill*

Whiting's model involves:

- **input from display:** what can be seen, heard etc.
- **receptor systems:** receive information from the senses via the sense organs
- **perceptual mechanisms:** perceive what has been received and selective attention occurs. This involves DCR (detect, compare, recognise) — detect what has been received, compare to past experiences, recognise what is important and what needs to be done
- **translatory mechanisms:** help to convert information into coded information that can be compared to the memory
- **effector mechanisms:** the network of nerves that sends coded impulses to the muscles with the desired response
- **muscular system output data:** information is received by the muscles to be acted upon
- **feedback data:** feedback is received about the decision that has been made

Reaction time, response time and anticipation

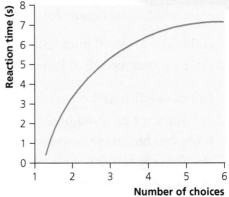

Figure 18 Hick's law

- **reaction time:** the time taken from the onset of a stimulus to the onset of a response (simple and choice)
- **movement time:** the time for which the athlete is moving, i.e. how long it has taken to complete the task (in terms of movement)
- **response time:** reaction time + movement time

Factors affecting response time

- Hick's law (reaction time increases as the number of choices increases, Figure 18)
- psychological refractory period (a delay when a second stimulus is presented before the first has been processed)
- single channel hypothesis (where only one stimulus can be processed at a time, Figure 19)
- fitness level
- anticipation

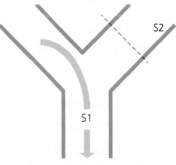

Figure 19 The single channel hypothesis: only one stimulus can be processed at a time

Strategies to improve response time

- making use of mental practice
- training to the specific stimulus expected in the performance situation
- learning to focus on picking up the stimulus more quickly
- improving aspects of fitness to improve response time
- more effective use of anticipation

Exam tip

If you are asked about anticipation, remember there are two types: pre-judging a stimulus and anticipating when it will happen is **temporal anticipation**; **spatial anticipation** refers to what is going to happen where.

Schmidt's schema theory

A schema is a basic set of commands that can be adapted to a situation.

Schmidt suggested that rather than use a structured set of movements to develop skills, the core principles can be taken from an existing motor programme and then adapted, using some information from the environment and by using feedback from the senses.

There are four pieces of information that allow schemas to develop. These four things are placed under two headings, recall schema and recognition schema (Figure 20).

Recall schema: stored information about how to produce a movement. Used before the movement.

1 **Initial conditions:** before we start, we work out where we are (environment) and where our limbs are, how tense certain muscles are etc.
2 **Response specification:** we work out our movement objective — which motor programme we want to recall in order to satisfy the situation, need, speed of the object, timing factors etc.

Recognition schema: during and after movement, this information allows the performer to evaluate how well their performance is going/went.

1 **Sensory consequences:** as we undertake the movement, we receive information from our muscles (kinaesthesia) about whether the movement feels correct or not.
2 **Response outcome:** this is when we compare the outcome of the movement to what we hoped it would do (objective).

Key terms

Recall schema Initiates movement, comes before the action

Recognition schema Controls the movement, how it feels and whether it was successful

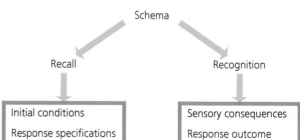

Figure 20 **Schema theory: a summary**

Developing the ability to build and adapt schemas

- as a child you must be given the opportunity to develop the skills to do basic things that you can then adapt at a later date, e.g. kick, throw, catch etc.
- you then need to be given the opportunity to experience varied practices so that you can learn how to adapt this information, e.g. catch small balls, big balls, different shapes, at different speeds etc.
- you first need to experience a correct movement, e.g. catch before you can detect whether the sensory consequences are correct

- you will initially need external feedback on your actions before developing kinaesthesia as you progress
- positive feedback should be given as you develop the ability to adapt the stored motor programme

Strategies to improve information processing

Information processing can be improved. Strategies can be employed to develop better decision making:

- concentrating on the input phase and making more effective use of the selective-attention decision-making process
- effectively using chunking (breaking the skilled action into parts or subroutines)
- chaining (linking new information with old, already used information so that multiple links can form a chain)
- improving reaction time through improved fitness

Exam tip

You should be able to apply the schema theory to specific sporting situations, so go through the parameters (essential processes) of this at least once for an identified and specified sporting situation.

Do you know?

1 What is Hick's law?
2 What four strategies can be used to improve information processing?
3 Schema theory uses two main schemas. What are they?

End of section 2 questions

1 What is meant by the term 'efficient'?
2 Name the four different methods of guidance.
3 Is a forward roll a simple or a complex skill?
4 What is meant by positive transfer of learning?
5 What is meant by negative transfer of learning?
6 What is meant by zero transfer of learning?
7 What is meant by bilateral transfer of learning?
8 What is meant by the 'whole–part–whole' way of presenting practice?
9 Why might a simple catch be taught using the whole method of presenting practice?
10 Summarise the three stages of learning.
11 Draw and label a basic information processing model.

3 Sport and society

3.1 Emergence of globalisation of sport in the twenty-first century

You need to know

- what society was like in Britain in the pre-industrial age (pre-1780) :
  - ☐ characteristics and impact on sporting recreation
  - ☐ characteristics of popular and rational recreation linked to the two-tier class system
- industrial and post-industrial (1780–1900) characteristics and impact on sport, limited to development of association football, lawn tennis, rationalisation of track and field events and the role of the Wenlock Olympian Games
- post-Second World War (1950–present) characteristics and impact on sport, limited to development of association football, tennis and athletics

Pre-industrial (pre-1780)

Socio-cultural factors about this period:

- transport and communication links were limited
- only the educated classes could read and write
- the lower classes worked long hours, dictated by the agricultural calendar
- the feudal system meant there was a strong class divide between the rich and poor
- sport mirrored aspects of society — the unruly working class tended to perform unruly pastimes, e.g. mob football

Popular recreation

Popular recreation refers to the sporting pastimes of people in pre-industrial Britain. Working hours were long and time was limited, so opportunities for participation tended to fall around festivals or holy days. Limited transport meant that activities were local and relevant to a small area. Participants made use of rural facilities, e.g. open land for mob games.

Exam tip

A basic understanding of the socio-cultural factors which prevailed during each period (pre-industrial, post-industrial and post-Second World War) will help to put this provision and development of sport into historical perspective.

Key term

The feudal system A method of structuring society based on a person's role, e.g. king, land owners, labourers/workers etc.

The two-tier class system was exemplified by the two activities of mob football and real tennis.

Mob football was an early form of football, which often used a pig's bladder as the ball. This game was localised and rural with virtually no rules or regulations. It tended to be male-dominated and violent.

Real tennis was not a typical popular recreation. It was a game played exclusively by the upper classes in purpose-built facilities, using specialised equipment and with a clear set of rules.

Rational recreation

Rational recreation involved sporting activities designed by the middle classes for the lower classes to play. The intention was that they would be organised, well-ordered and controlled, as previous sporting pastimes had tended to involve gambling, violence, damage to properties, injury and death.

Sporting pastimes had to 'move with the times' and as Britain industrialised, sport became more organised and less unruly.

Industrial and post-industrial (1780–1900)
The Industrial Revolution

The **Industrial Revolution** occurred during the mid-eighteenth to the mid-nineteenth centuries. This period marked a change in Britain from a feudal, rural society into an industrialised, machine-based, capitalist society, controlled by a powerful urban middle class.

Impact of the Industrial Revolution

The first half of the nineteenth century saw many negative effects:
- much of the population moved from the countryside into towns and cities for improved employment opportunities and amenities
- space in cities was sparse and there was poor health and hygiene
- there was a lack of public facilities and wages were low

However, the second half of the nineteenth century saw:
- improvements in health and hygiene
- gradual increases in wages and time available for leisure
- the development of a middle class, who gave some time for their workers to play sport

> ## Exam tip
>
> Remember the three **Ls** when thinking about mob football:
> Literacy was low so rules were not written or followed.
> **L**ower class played mob football.
> **L**ocal — mob football was played locally.

- the growing value of 'athleticism'
- the set-up of factory sports teams. **Industrial patronage** helped factory owners to encourage loyalty through sporting provision

Transport, communication and urbanisation

- the invention of the steam engine led to the railway network being built. Consequently the postal service became far more efficient
- newspapers developed as printing techniques developed. People could therefore read about sport in newspapers
- travel was cheaper and more accessible so people could travel to watch and play sport
- urbanisation encouraged further movement of the population from the countryside into towns and cities

The British Empire

At its height, the British Empire was the largest empire in history and at that time was the foremost global power. By 1921, it ruled approximately one-quarter of the world's surface. Due to this, the British development of sport also spread throughout the empire, particularly specific sports and organisational influences:

- army officers played sport and spread concepts overseas
- the clergy took sport overseas as part of their missionary work
- diplomats tended to travel and encourage sports like rugby and cricket

Increased emphasis on leisure

Provision made through factories, churches and local authorities all encouraged and endorsed sport, especially organised versions. Churches set up church teams, factories set up factory teams, e.g. Cadbury Athletic Football Club. Football was commonly played at the end of the nineteenth century.

Three-tier class system

- emergence of self-made middle class had empathy with the working class
- codified rules for sport were developed
- competitions were set up
- philanthropists helped to build public facilities, e.g. public baths and parks
- gradually gave the working class more leisure time
- helped to develop 'professional' sports people

Key terms

Urbanisation The transformation of rural, low-population areas into highly populated, urban areas

Codification The emergence of stated rules for sports

Development of national governing bodies

- **national governing bodies** began to emerge as sport became more organised (see Figure 21)
- bodies were set up to deal with structure, competition and leagues, e.g. the Football Association in 1863
- the middle and upper classes wanted to maintain control and national governing bodies were a means of doing that

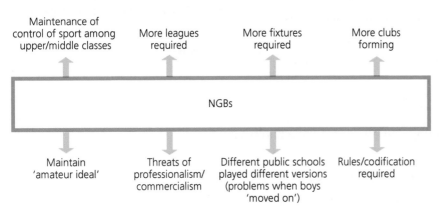

Figure 21 Factors affecting the formation of NGBs

Characteristics and impact of sport

Rational recreation characterised post-industrial sport (Figure 22 and Table 10).

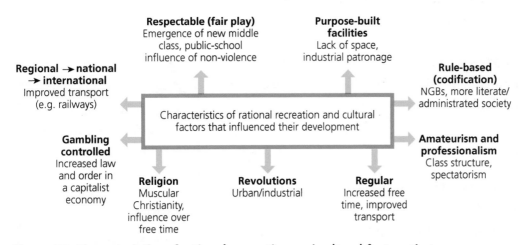

Figure 22 Characteristics of rational recreation and cultural factors that influenced their development

Table 10 **Factors affecting the development of sports**

Association football	Lawn tennis	Track and field athletics
Urbanisation	Middle class aspiring to be like upper class	Became popular in crowded urban areas
Increased professionalism		Purpose-built tracks
Middle-class approval	Lawned/hedged areas purpose built	Upper/middle class ran for enjoyment
Increased organisation, e.g. the FA	Private clubs	Lower class ran for money-wagering
Better transport links for teams and spectators	Organised by middle class	Amateur Athletic Association formed in 1866 (excluded working class)
Better media coverage	Standardised rules (Wingfield)	Amateur Athletic Association (AAA) formed in 1880 (inclusive of working class)
Greater disposable income for spectators	Specialist equipment	
	Played by males and females	Initially women were excluded (unladylike)

Wenlock Olympic Games

■ the Wenlock Agricultural Reading Society wanted to establish an Olympian class
■ intended to promote intellectual, moral and physical improvements (in the working class in particular)
■ included games of athletics, country sports and fun events
■ influenced and inspired Baron de Coubertin in his reform of the modern Olympic games

Changing role of women in sport

■ approval of female sporting endeavour slowly grew
■ suburban middle-class women took part in lawn tennis wearing a 'bustle skirt'
■ 1884 saw the first Ladies Singles Championship at Wimbledon
■ private-school girls started to take part in athletic activities, including track and field

Amateur and professional performers

■ the nineteenth-century concept of the **gentleman amateur** applied solely to the middle and upper class
■ gentleman amateurs played a range of sports, displayed a high moral code, were respected and were wealthy so had free time
■ lower classes had to be paid a wage to play sport (professionals)
■ earning money from sport was seen as a way out of poverty (social mobility)

Key terms

Amateur A person who plays sport purely for the love of it

Professional A person who plays sport for money or extrinsic gain

Gentleman amateur Middle or upper-class performer showing high levels of morals

Table 11 **Comparing characteristics of amateurs with professionals**

Key characteristics of amateurs	Key characteristics of professionals
Middle and upper class only	Lower class
Played a range of sports	Played to earn money
Wanted to be seen as displaying a high moral code	Played to rise out of poverty
Used free time to play	Played to rise through class system and social standings
Wanted to be seen as 'gentlemen amateurs'	Paid for by the middle and upper classes

Exam tip

Do not confuse the point that the middle/upper classes were amateur and the lower classes were professional.

Post-Second World War (1950–present)

There have been considerable developments in the nature of sport since 1950, including the emergence of more female performers and the important role played by the media.

The golden triangle

The golden triangle is the interrelationship between commercialisation (including sponsorship), media (radio, television, satellite, internet and social media), and sports and governing bodies (Figure 23).

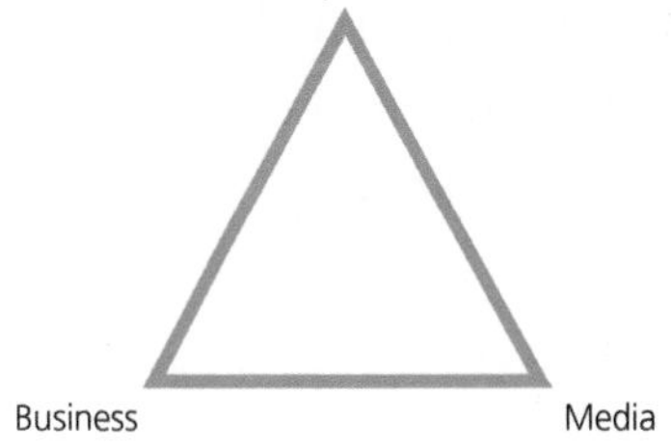

The media is effectively an organised means of communication, which includes radio, television, newspapers, internet and social media, by which large numbers of people can be reached quickly. Thus, sponsorship is closely linked to media as it increases the possibilities of commercialism to attempt to gain money from an activity such as sport.

Social media is easily the fastest growing aspect of the media at present. This also relates to increased globalisation, whereby nations are increasingly being linked together and people are becoming more interdependent via these improvements in communication and travel.

Each element of the triangle relies heavily on the other, e.g. high levels of sponsorship are only made available if there is a high level of media coverage to make it financially viable.

Figure 23 **The 'golden triangle'**

Key terms

Golden triangle The relationship between sport, business and the media

Sponsorship Where a company pays for their products to be publicly displayed or advertised in an attempt to increase the sales of their goods

Social media Online apps and websites which allow users to interact by sharing content and taking part in social networking

Commercialisation of sport

Commercialised sport involves:
- a focus on professionals
- sport being seen as part of the entertainment industry

- athletes being seen as commodities
- a lot of media coverage
- performers getting paid more
- performers becoming famous
- performers being controlled by their sponsors
- rules occasionally being changed to make the sport more entertaining
- associations between brands and performers
- merchandising of goods

Amateur and professional performers

- the advent of 'open sport' meant both amateurs and professionals could compete against each other (blurring of amateur/ professional status)
- professionals are now of a higher status
- some amateurs receive expense payments to train and travel
- amateurs are still encouraged to perform fairly (by the rules and according to high moral standards)
- pressures on professionals sometimes leads to negative deviance, e.g. drug-taking, cheating etc.

Elite female performers

Football

- emergence of female-only leagues
- females as players, officials and coaches
- more female role models
- better media coverage
- increased grassroots participation

Tennis

- emergence of the Women's Tennis Association (WTA)
- development of women's circuit to play in
- increased prize money available
- more female role models

Athletics

- increased opportunities for women to participate
- emergence of more Olympic and World Championship events for women
- increased coverage of female athletics
- emergence of role models, e.g. (late twentieth and early twenty-first centuries) Jessica Ennis-Hill (Olympian) and Dame Tanni Grey-Thompson (Paralympian)

> **Exam tip**
>
> This topic includes 'to present' and there are many factors included which are changing almost daily, so it is important to keep your knowledge up-to-date.

> **Key term**
>
> Merchandising The practice in which the brand or image from one product is used to sell another, e.g. professional sports teams/ performers promoting various products

> **Exam tip**
>
> This topic is one where you are likely to be asked to understand, interpret and analyse data and graphs relating to participation in physical activity and sport.

3.2 Impact of sport on society and of society on sport

You need to know

- definitions of the following key terms in relation to the study of sport and their impact on equal opportunities in sport and society: society, socialisation, social processes, social issues, social structures/stratification
- social action theory in relation to social issues in physical activity and sport
- underrepresented groups in sport
- the terms equal opportunities, discrimination, stereotyping and prejudice
- the barriers to participation in sport and physical activity and possible solutions to overcome them for underrepresented groups in sport
- benefits of raising participation
- the interrelationship between Sport England, local and national partners to increase participation at grassroots level and in underrepresented groups in sport

Sociological theory applied to equal opportunities

Society is an organised group of people associated for some specific purpose or with a shared common interest. There are various terms that you should be able to describe.

Socialisation

This is a lifelong process where members of a society learn its norms, values, ideas, practices and roles in order to take their place in that society. This is further divided into:

- **primary socialisation** (the early years of childhood taking place largely within the family). Families teach basic values and acceptable behavioural norms. This may include the acceptance of physical exercise as a norm
- **secondary socialisation**, which occurs during later years as teenagers and adults. Peer groups and school heavily influence behaviour and accepted norms. For example, high standards of manners and sporting endeavour

Social processes

Social control is the process of attempting to control people's thoughts, appearance, feelings and behaviour. In sport this could include how people are expected to dress and behave when performing. Linked to this are the causes and consequences of inequality.

Social change is a change in the way society is organised. From a sporting perspective this could include sport becoming more accessible for minority groups or for people with disabilities. Another example is that of the 'This Girl Can' campaign which aims to encourage more women to take part in sporting activities.

Social issues

Social issues must be considered as these are problems that affect many people within a society. It is useful to remember:

Social inequality

- social inequality occurs when resources and opportunities are not evenly spread through the different social classes or genders
- there is an unequal distribution of wealth
- there can be differences in the wages of men and women performing the same roles
- some of the inequalities can be caused by money, role models (or a lack of), stereotypes and levels of confidence (which may be low)

Social stratification and social class

- a way of dividing up members of society based on characteristics such as wealth or status
- those at the top tend to have greater wealth and opportunities
- Sport England targets members of society they feel are 'underrepresented'
- those attending public, fee-paying schools often have better facilities available for sport
- research suggests that those of a lower social status often (but not always) have poorer health and a lower level of physical activity

Social action theory

- this is a way of viewing socialisation, emphasising social action, to include the interactionist approach
- sport has moved and changed with the dynamics in society, i.e. it is not static
- sport has and is sometimes used to gain equality, e.g. women not being stereotyped in a domestic role
- social action involves an action being carried out by an individual to which they attach meaning, e.g. starting a new sports club
- starting a women's club in a traditional men's sport
- social action may involve creativity that is followed in social circles and may be slightly different to the perceived norm, e.g. Dick Fosbury performed a 'Fosbury flop' which was then copied by others who understood its value when high-jumping
- sport has affected society and society has affected sport

> ### Key term
>
> **Interactionist approach**
> The study of how people behave within a society and through socialisation

Barriers to participation

Barriers exist in society which prevent or lessen the potential for certain groups to participate. These barriers tend to be time, money, motivation, skill and prejudice.

The main unrepresented groups in sport are:

- people with disabilities (where impairment adversely affects performance)
- ethnic minorities (people who have racial, religious or linguistic traits in common)
- gender disadvantaged (relating to the biological aspect of a person, whether male or female)

Table 12 **Barriers to participation**

People with disabilities	Ethnic minorities	Women
Lack of role models	Racism/racist abuse	Lack of time and money
Inaccessible facilities	Religious observances/culture	School PE programmes (fewer options)
Lack of specialist coaches/ equipment	Fewer role models (e.g. among coaches)	Fewer sponsorship opportunities/less funding
Stereotypes	Fear of rejection/lack of self-esteem	Stereotypical myths
Lack of organised competition		Fewer role models
Low levels of media coverage		Less media coverage

Strategies to prevent barriers to participation are relatively common to all groups (Table 13).

Table 13

Underrepresented group	Strategies to prevent barriers to participation
People with disabilities	■ more investment
	■ increased media coverage
Ethnic minorities	■ promotion of role models
	■ structured competitions
Women	■ train more coaches (of ethnic minority/people with disabilities /women)
	■ campaigns to encourage participation
	■ adapt competitions/facilities, e.g. disability-friendly, female changing areas

Stereotyping and prejudice

Stereotyping is to create a standardised image of all members of a group, allowing others to categorise and treat them unfairly, e.g. negative stereotypes about women which negatively impact on their participation in sport/physical activity.

Prejudice is to form an unfavourable opinion of an individual, often based on inadequate facts (such as a lack of tolerance for or a dislike of people from a specific race, religion or culture). This can negatively affect a person's treatment of a performer.

These factors have often discouraged participation, but they can be offset by the benefits of raising participation, which include:
- physical benefits (living longer and less likelihood of disease)
- fitness benefits (components of fitness can be improved)
- social benefits (social and emotional health can be improved)

Key terms

Stereotyping Simple (sometimes uninformed) generalisations about all members of a group which allow others to categorise and treat them (potentially) unfairly

Prejudice Bias against an individual or group based on personal or unjustified opinions

Reasons for raising participation

There are many reasons for encouraging participation in sport, and these can be divided into physical, fitness and social factors (Table 14).

Table 14 Reasons for increasing participation

Physical	Fitness	Social
Improved levels of health Less chance of developing disease Reduce strain on the NHS	Improved levels of fitness Improved work productivity	Increased socialisation Social control Creation of jobs Positive use of free time

The role of Sport England

Sport England has a vision that everyone, no matter what their background and characteristics, can take part in physical activity. Its work and strategy can be summarised as:

- 'towards an active nation'
- a national body, working with national and local partners and the underrepresented groups in sport, at grassroots level
- promotion of the benefits of being active
- investment in county sports partnerships
- coordinated approach with national governing bodies to promote participation and develop talent, including Whole Sport Plans

In 2018, Sport England worked with a number of nationally funded partners to develop a coordinated approach to encourage participation (Table 15).

> **Key term**
>
> **Whole Sport Plans** A report submitted to Sport England, which details how national governing bodies plan to invest money to increase participation

Table 15

Nationally funded partner	Aim
Sporting Equals	Promotion of participation within disadvantaged communities, most noticeably black and ethnic minorities
English Federation of Disability Sport (EFDS)	To increase participation among people with disabilities (charity organisation)
Women in Sport	To increase participation rates of women in sport

> **Exam tip**
>
> The role of Sport England and the links it has with national and local partners is an important one in relation to increased participation levels, so it requires greater depth of study.

Sport England has launched many campaigns to promote participation. Two examples are given below.

'This Girl Can'

This campaign targets women and aims to tell a realistic story about exercise, i.e. women will jiggle and sweat! It aims to move away from idealised and stylised images of how women are portrayed in the media to one which is more realistic.

3 Sport and society

'Get Yourself Active'

This is a programme which involves health, social care and sports sector partners working together to develop better opportunities for people with disabilities.

Do you know?

1 What are the main underrepresented groups in sport?
2 What role does Sport England play in helping to raise levels of participation in sport?
3 State three social benefits of aiming to increase participation rates.
4 What is meant by stereotyping?

End of section 3 questions

1 State three characteristics of pre-industrial Britain.
2 State three characteristics of commercialisation in sport.
3 What term describes an unequal distribution of wealth and opportunity within society?
4 Suggest four strategies to encourage underrepresented groups to participate more in physical activity.
5 What term can be described as 'giving people access to facilities and opportunities irrespective of factors such as race, age, sex, mental or physical capability'?
6 What theory can explain an action by individual that may not fully conform to society's norms, which they believe has meaning?

52   Need to know: AQA A-level PE

4 Exercise physiology and biomechanics

4.1 Diet and nutrition

You need to know
- the exercise-related function of food classes
- positive and negative effects of dietary supplements and their manipulation of the performer

Food classes

A balanced diet is essential for optimum performance. A balanced diet consists of the seven classes of food detailed below.

Carbohydrates

- consist of simple and complex carbohydrates
- simple carbohydrates are found in fruits
- complex carbohydrates are found in nearly all plant-based foods, the most common being bread, pasta, rice and vegetables
- the principal source of energy used by the body
- once digested, they are converted to glucose
- glucose can then be stored in the muscles and liver as glycogen

Fats

- there are three types of fat:
  - □ saturated fats (found in sweet and savoury foods)
  - □ trans-fat (a type of unsaturated fat found in meat and dairy products)
  - □ cholesterol (a type of fat that circulates in the body)
- used during low intensity exercise as a provider of energy

Proteins

- made up of a specific combination of chemicals called amino acids
- important for muscle growth and repair
- sources of protein include meat, fish, eggs and dairy products

Key terms

Glucose A simple sugar and a major source of energy for body cells

Glycogen The stored form of glucose found in muscle and liver cells

Amino acids Chemical compounds used in all body cells to build proteins

Table 16 **The exercise-related role of carbohydrates, fats and proteins**

Food class	Exercise-related function
Carbohydrate	Principal source of energy for both low intensity (aerobic) and high intensity (anaerobic) exercise. They are the only food source that can be broken down anaerobically, e.g. the 200-metre race is an anaerobic event.
Fat	Used for long duration, low intensity exercise such as marathons.
Protein	Minor source of energy and tend to be used more by power athletes who have a greater need to repair and develop muscle tissue.

Vitamins

- essential nutrients that your body needs in small amounts in order to work properly
- there are two types of vitamin: fat-soluble and water-soluble

The list of vitamins you need to be aware of is limited to Table 17.

Table 17

Vitamin	Source	Exercise-related function
C (ascorbic acid)	Green vegetables, fruit	Protects cells and keeps them healthy. Helps in the maintenance of bones, teeth, gums and connective tissue such as ligaments.
D	Sunlight (greatest source), oily fish, dairy products (lesser source)	Has a role in the absorption of calcium, which keeps bones and teeth healthy.
B1 (thiamin)	Yeast, eggs, liver, wholegrain bread, nuts, red meat, cereals	Works with other B-group vitamins to help break down and release energy from food. Keeps the nervous system healthy.
B2 (riboflavin)	Dairy products, liver, vegetables, eggs, cereals, fruit	Works with other B-group vitamins to help break down and release energy from food. Keeps the skin, eyes, and nervous system healthy.
B6	Meat, fish, eggs, bread, vegetables, cereals	Helps form haemoglobin. Helps the body to use and store energy from protein and carbohydrate in food.
B12 (folate)	Red meat, dairy products, fish	Makes red blood cells and keeps the nervous system healthy. Releases energy from food.

Minerals

- these assist in bodily functions
- they include sodium (which helps to regulate fluid levels in the body)
- they also include iron (which helps in the formation of haemoglobin in red blood cells to transport oxygen)
- they also include calcium (the need for strong bones and teeth and is also necessary for efficient nerve and muscle function)

Fibre

- found in wholemeal bread and pasta, potatoes, nuts, seeds, fruit, vegetables and pulses
- insoluble fibre can speed up digestion and prevent constipation

Water

- important for hydration before, during and after exercise
- necessary to prevent dehydration

Key terms

Hydration Having enough water to enable normal functioning of the body

Dehydration Where the body is losing more fluid than it is taking in

Dietary supplements

Dietary supplements can be used to artificially manipulate performance, but these have both positive and negative effects.

Creatine

A compound the body can make naturally which supplies energy for muscular contraction. It can also be used as a supplement to increase athletic performance (Table 18).

Table 18 **Advantages and disadvantages of creatine supplementation**

Positive effects	Negative effects
Aims to provide ATP Replenishes phosphocreatine stores Allows the ATP–PC system to last longer Improves muscle mass	Possible side effects include muscle cramps, diarrhoea, water retention, bloating, vomiting Hinders aerobic performance Mixed evidence to show benefits

Sodium bicarbonate

A white, soluble compound used as an antacid. See Table 19.

Table 19 **Advantages and disadvantages of taking sodium bicarbonate**

Positive effects	Negative effects
Reduces acidity in the muscle cells Delays fatigue Increases the buffering capacity of the blood	Possible side effects include vomiting, pain, cramping, diarrhoea, bloating

Caffeine

A naturally occurring stimulant which increases alertness and reduces fatigue. See Table 20.

Table 20 **Advantages and disadvantages of taking caffeine**

Positive effects	Negative effects
Stimulant/increased mental alertness	Loss of fine control
Reduces effects of fatigue	Against rules of most sports in large quantities
Allows fats to be used as an energy source/delays use of glycogen stores	Possible side effects include dehydration, insomnia, muscle cramps, stomach cramps, vomiting, irregular heartbeat, diarrhoea
Improves decision making/improves reaction time	
May benefit aerobic performance/endurance athletes	

Glycogen loading

A form of dietary manipulation used by endurance athletes to increase glycogen stores beyond that which can normally be stored. See Table 21.

Table 21 **Advantages and disadvantages of glycogen loading**

Positive effects	Negative effects
Increased glycogen storage	During the carbo-loading phase: ■ water retention, which results in bloating ■ heavy legs ■ affects digestion ■ weight increase
Increased glycogen stores in the muscle	
Delays fatigue	
Increases endurance capacity	During the depletion phase: ■ irritability ■ can alter the training programme through a lack of energy

Do you know?

1 What are the seven classes of food?
2 What energy source is used at medium to high intensity exercise?
3 What energy sources are used at low intensity exercise?

4.2 Preparation and training methods

You need to know

- key data terms for laboratory conditions and field tests
- physiological effects and benefits of a warm up and cool down
- principles of training
- application of principles of periodisation
- training methods to improve physical fitness and health

Make sure you are aware of the definitions of the following key terms for laboratory conditions and field tests.

Key terms

Quantitative Can be written down or measured with numbers

Qualitative Descriptive and looks at the way people think or feel, perhaps from an interview

Objective Involving facts

Subjective Involving opinions

Validity When the test actually measures what it sets out to do

Reliability The test can be repeated accurately and give similar results

Warm up and cool down

A warm up generally involves:
- pulse-raising exercises, e.g. jogging
- stretching
- skill-based/familiarisation movements and skills

Cooling down usually involves:
- exercises to maintain heart rate initially
- gradual reduction in heart rate and breathing rate
- stretching

Completing a warm up and a cool down has many benefits (Table 22).

Table 22 Benefits of a warm up and cool down

Benefits of a warm up	Benefits of a cool down
Muscle temperature increases	Removal of lactic acid
Reaction time decreases/gets faster	Reduced chances of DOMS
Injury chances reduce	Maintains venous return
Increased movement at the joints	Gradually reduces temperature
Psychological preparation	
Movements are rehearsed	
More oxygen to the working muscles	

Key terms

DOMS Delayed onset of muscle soreness

Overload The gradual increase in stress placed on the body during exercise training that is more than normal

Principles of training

This can be summarised with the acronym 'SPORR':

Specificity: making training specific to the sport being played/movements used/muscles used/energy systems used.

Progressive Overload: gradual increase in the amount of overload so that fitness gains occur but without potential for injury.

Reversibility: losing fitness levels when you stop exercising.

Recovery: rest is required in appropriate amounts.

Principles of overload

To improve performance you need to train more, harder, longer and with the correct type of training. This can be summarised with the acronym 'FITT':

Frequency: how often?

Intensity: how hard?

Time: how long for?

Type: of training?

Principles of periodisation

Periodisation is the method of dividing the training year into specific sections for specific purposes. These sections can be cycles:
- **macrocycle** (a long-term training goal)
- **mesocycle** (usually a 4–12 week period of training with a particular focus)
- **microcycle** (a week or a few days of training)

A macrocycle can be divided up into periods:
- **preparation:** similar to pre-season training where fitness is developed
- **competition:** the performance period where skills and techniques are refined and fitness is maintained

- **transition/rest:** the end of the season where rest and recovery take place and light aerobic training may take place

When dividing the year up into sections, the concepts of **tapering** and **peaking** are key to an athlete's success.

- **tapering:** reducing the volume and/or intensity of training prior to competition
- **peaking:** planning and organising training so a performer is at their peak, both physically and mentally, for a major competition. Performers can aim for a double-peak, e.g. World Championships followed by Olympic Games

Table 23 Training methods used to improve physical fitness and health

Name of training method	Description
Continuous training	Working continuously to develop aerobic power and cardiovascular endurance. Long exercise periods without rest at a relatively steady state, e.g. jogging, swimming, rowing etc.
Interval training	Generally used to improve anaerobic power. Involves periods of high intensity work with periods of rest. Involves a work to rest ratio.
Fartlek (speed-play)	Generally used to improve the aerobic energy system but can also improve the anaerobic. Varying the intensity and terrain of exercise.
Circuit training (Figure 24)	A circuit can be designed to work on aerobic or anaerobic systems. Involves periods of work at 'stations' interspersed with periods of rest. The stations can be designed to be specific to a sport.

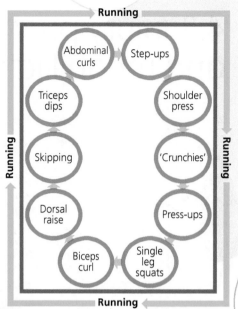

Figure 24 An example of a circuit

Proprioceptive neuromuscular facilitation (PNF)

PNF is a type of passive stretching to improve the range of movement at a joint (flexibility), which involves:

- isometric contraction for at least ten seconds
- period of relaxation
- stretch further

4.3 Injury prevention and rehabilitation

You need to know

- types of injury, including:
  - ☐ acute (fractures, dislocations, strains, sprains)
  - ☐ chronic (Achilles tendonitis, stress fracture, 'tennis elbow')
- different methods used in injury prevention, rehabilitation and recovery
- physiological reasons for methods used in injury rehabilitation
- importance of sleep and nutrition for improved recovery

Types of injury

Any form of injury effectively reduces the efficiency of part of a body system, so being aware of how to prevent injuries is crucial for optimal performance.

Acute injuries, are sudden, caused by a specific impact or traumatic event where a sharp pain is felt immediately. These include:

- **fractures:** a break or crack in the bone
- **dislocations:** when the ends of the bones are forced out of position; occurs only at joints
- **strains:** a pulled or 'torn' muscle; when muscle fibres are stretched too far and tear
- **sprains:** when excessive force is applied to a joint and the ligament stretches and tears; occurs to ligaments at the joints

Chronic injuries are often referred to as over-use injuries. These include:

- **Achilles tendonitis:** where the Achilles tendon (located at the back of the ankle) is inflamed, causing pain
- **stress fracture:** the area becomes tender and swollen; this is most common in the weight-bearing bones of the legs
- **tennis elbow:** occurring in the muscles attached to the elbow that are used to straighten the wrist; when the muscles and tendons become inflamed and tiny tears occur on the outside of the elbow

Key terms

Acute injuries Injuries caused by a specific impact or traumatic events

Chronic injuries Injuries caused through over-use

Injury prevention

Methods of injury prevention include:

- **screening**, which is any form of testing to detect abnormalities or medical conditions, e.g. heart or musculoskeletal conditions
- **protective equipment**, e.g. shin pads
- **warm up** (see 'Warm up and cool down' on page 57)
- **flexibility training** (active, passive, static, ballistic)
- **taping** (as simple as taping up vulnerable or damaged areas)
- **bracing** (such as knee and ankle braces)

Injury rehabilitation

Methods of injury rehabilitation include:

- **proprioceptive training**, which uses hopping, jumping and balance exercises to restore lost proprioception and teach the body to control the position of an injured joint subconsciously
- **strength training**, to re-strengthen the injured area
- **hyperbaric chambers**, which are pressurised chambers that contain 100% pure oxygen, so that more oxygen can be breathed in and therefore diffused to the injured area
- **cryotherapy**, the use of cold temperatures to treat an injury
- **hydrotherapy**, which takes place in warm water and is used to improve blood circulation, relieve pain and relax muscles

Recovery from exercise

Methods to enhance and speed up recovery from exercise include:

- **compression garments:** used to improve blood circulation and prevent medical problems such as deep vein thrombosis (DVT)
- **massage:** involves kneading and rubbing muscles to increase the blood flow to the injured area and to break down scar tissue, while removing tension and lactic acid
- **foam rollers:** act in the same way as massage
- **cold therapy:** cooling the skin by applying ice to give pain relief and decrease blood flow to reduce any bleeding or swelling
- **ice baths:** involve entering iced water for a few minutes. The cold causes blood vessels to the muscles to vasoconstrict and the body's core receives most of the blood. After leaving the ice bath the vessels vasodilate, allowing oxygen-rich blood to flush the muscles or injured area

Sleep and nutrition

After exercise, the body must have enough time to recover and replenish lots stores. The general rule is to get 7–9 hours of sleep per night, but the quality of the sleep is also important. During sleep, glycogen stores may be replenished from food consumed, and ingested protein helps with muscle repair.

Synoptic link

Rehabilitation requires some knowledge of the section of the specification called 'Diet and nutrition'.

Do you know?

1 What type of injury is an over-use injury?
2 Which type of rehabilitation method uses very cold temperatures?
3 Which recovery method uses rubbing and kneading?

4.4 Biomechanical principles, levers and linear motion

You need to know

- Newton's three laws of linear motion applied to sporting movements
- definitions, equations and units of example scalars (biomechanical principles)
- centre of mass
- factors affecting stability
- three classes of lever and examples of their use in the body
- mechanical advantage and mechanical disadvantage of each class of lever
- the forces acting on a performer during linear motion
- definitions, equations and units of vectors and scalars (linear motion)
- the relationship between impulse and increasing and decreasing momentum in sprinting through the interpretation of force/time graphs

Biomechanical principles

Newton's three laws of linear motion

Law of inertia

Newton's first law states that:

'Every body continues in its state of rest or uniform motion in a straight line unless compelled to change that state by a large enough external force which overcomes its inertia'.

For example, a golf ball will remain on the tee unless a force is applied by a golf club.

Law of acceleration

Newton's second law states that:

force (F) = mass (m) × acceleration (a)

If a large enough force is applied, then an object will:
- accelerate in the direction of the force
- accelerate in proportion to the amount of force applied

'The rate of momentum/acceleration of a body is proportional to the force causing it and occurs in the direction of the force.'

Law of action/reaction

Newton's third law refers to action and subsequent reaction (forces). This may be a ground reaction force (GRF) to push off of the ground.

'For every action there is an equal and opposite reaction.'

For example, a swimmer provides the action force towards a wall when turning and receives back an equal and opposite reaction force to push off the wall.

> ## Key terms
>
> **Force** Strength or energy which causes movement
>
> **Inertia** The resistance an object has to a change in its state of motion
>
> **Acceleration** Increasing in speed
>
> **Ground reaction force (GRF)** The equal and opposite force exerted on a performer who applies muscular force to the ground

> ## Exam tips
>
> - You need to be able to apply Newton's three laws of linear motion to sporting movements.
> - The application of Newton's laws can relate to any sporting object/body moving in a linear fashion. Thus, the laws stay the same and the application is changed to the object/body.

Table 24 **Newton's laws, applied to football**

Newton's laws	Application
Law of inertia	In a penalty, the ball (body) will remain on the spot (in a state of rest) unless it is kicked by the player (an external force is exerted upon it).
Law of acceleration	When the player kicks (force) the ball, the acceleration of the ball (rate of change of momentum) is proportional to the size of the force. So, the harder the ball is kicked, the further and faster it will go in the direction in which the force has been applied.
Law of action/reaction	When a footballer jumps up (action) to win a header, a force is exerted on the ground in order to gain height. At the same time, the ground exerts an upward force (equal and opposite reaction) upon the player.

Example scalars

You need to know the following definitions, equations and units. Scalar quantities refer to a measurement based on size only.

Speed is the rate of change of position, calculated as speed in metres per second ($m\,s^{-1}$).

Distance is the length of the path a body follows when moving from one position to another.

Each can be calculated using the equation:

$$\text{speed, } v \text{ (m s}^{-1}) = \frac{\text{distance covered in metres (m)}}{\text{time taken in seconds (s)}}$$

Centre of mass

The centre of mass is the point of balance of a body, or the point of concentration of mass. It tends to be in the middle of the body (hip area) but does move depending on the position of the body (Figure 25).

Factors affecting stability

Stability refers to how stable something is, i.e. how easy its state can be altered or moved.

Stability is affected by several factors:
- height of the centre of mass (lower is more stable)
- area of the base of the support (the wider it is, the more stable it is)
- position of the line of gravity (the more central the line extending vertically from the centre of mass and body mass, the better the stability)
- mass of the performer (the greater the mass, the greater its stability)

For example, a rugby player with a large mass will aim to adopt a low position with a wide stance when scrummaging to maintain stability.

Levers

Three classes of levers operate in the body during physical activity and sport:
1. **First-class lever:** the fulcrum lies between the effort and resistance. An example is during triceps extension (Figure 26).

Synoptic link box

Synoptic link

The concept of scalars links to the use of technology in data collection (quantitative and qualitative, objective and subjective, validity and reliability of data).

Figure 25 Centre of mass

Key terms

Fulcrum The point about which the lever rotates

Effort The use applied by the user/muscle of the lever arm

Resistance The weight applied to be moved by the muscle

2 **Second-class lever:** the resistance is between the fulcrum and effort. This lever is used during plantar flexion Figure 27.
3 **Third-class lever:** the effort is between the fulcrum and the resistance. This lever is used during the upwards phase of a biceps curl (Figure 28) or during leg flexion at the knee.

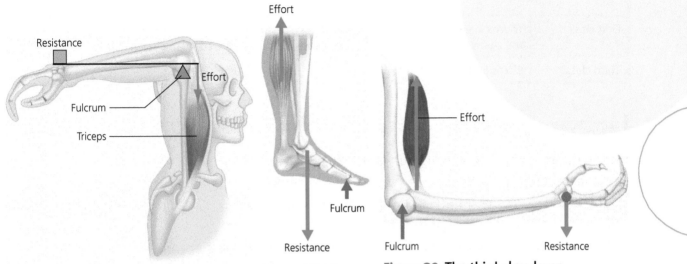

Figure 26 The first-class lever system at the elbow joint

Figure 27 The second-class lever system at the ankle joint

Figure 28 The third-class lever system at the elbow joint

Mechanical advantage refers to where the effort (force) arm is longer than the resistance arm. Mechanical advantage is highest at the second-class lever, although it does have a limited range of movement.

Mechanical disadvantage refers to where the resistance arm is longer than the effort (force) arm (Figure 29). A third-class lever cannot apply much force to move an object.

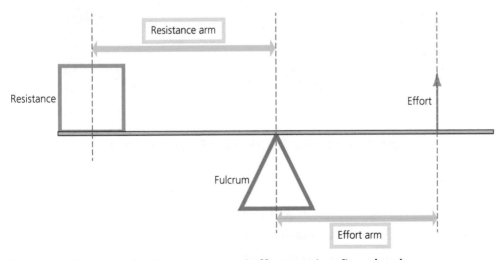

Figure 29 The idea of resistance arm and effort arm in a first-class lever

Table 25 Types of lever

Type of lever	Example	Mechanical advantage	Mechanical disadvantage
Second class	Plantar flexion of the ankle	Can generate much larger forces. Has to lift the whole body weight.	Slow, with a limited range of movement.
First class	Triceps in extension of the elbow	Large range of movement and any resistance can be moved quickly.	Cannot apply much force to move an object.
Third class	Biceps in flexion of the arm		

Linear motion

During linear motion (e.g. running forwards) there are varying forces that act on a performer:

- **gravity:** the force that attracts a body towards the centre of the Earth or towards any other physical body having mass
- **frictional force:** static frictional force is the force exerted on one surface by another where there is no motion between the two surfaces. Sliding frictional force is when dry friction acts between two surfaces that are moving relative to one another
- **air resistance:** a force that acts in the opposite direction to the motion of a body moving through the air
- **internal-muscular force:** force generated by the skeletal muscles
- **weight:** mass × acceleration, measured in newtons (N)
- **reaction force:** the result of an action force

Weight and reaction are the two vertical forces (Figure 30a and b).

Air resistance and gravity are the two horizontal forces (Figure 30c and d).

   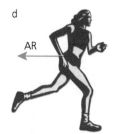

Figure 30 Free body diagrams. W = weight, R = resistance, F = friction, AR = air resistance

Vectors and scalars

You need to know the following definitions, equations and units. As mentioned previously, scalar quantities refer to a measurement based on size only, whereas vector quantities have both size and direction.

- **mass:** the quality of matter the body possesses (e.g. bone, muscle, fat, tissue, fluid)
- **weight:** measured in Newtons (N), the amount of gravity applied to mass. Calculated as mass (kg) × gravity (9.8)
- **speed:** distance ÷ time, the rate of change over a distance. Generally measured in metres per second ($m\,s^{-1}$) or miles per hour (mph)
- **velocity:** measured in metres per second ($m\,s^{-1}$), the rate of displacement (how fast a body travels in a given direction) (Figure 31). Calculated as displacement (m) ÷ time (s)

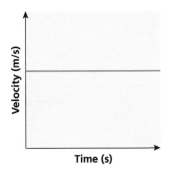

In this graph the gradient remains constant which indicates the performer is travelling at a constant velocity.

Now the gradient gets steeper (increases). This indicates that the performer is moving with increasing velocity or accelerating.

$$\text{gradient of graph} = \frac{\text{change in velocity}}{\text{time}}$$

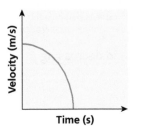

In this graph the gradient decreases. This shows the performer or object is moving with decreasing velocity or decelerating.

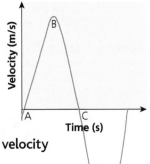

In this graph from A–B there is a positive curve above the x axis so the performer is accelerating. From B–C there is a negative curve so the performer is decelerating. At C the curve goes below the x axis which means there has been a change in direction.

Figure 31 Velocity–time graphs showing constant velocity and increasing velocity

- **distance displacement:** measured in metres (m), this is the shortest route in a straight line between the starting and finishing positions
- **acceleration:** measured in $m\,s^{-2}$, this is the rate of change of velocity (a vector quantity). Calculated as change of velocity ($m\,s^{-1}$) ÷ time (s)
- **momentum:** the product of the mass and velocity of an object, calculated by momentum ($kg\,m\,s^{-1}$) = mass (kg) × velocity ($m\,s^{-1}$)

Impulse and momentum

This topic covers the relation between impulse and increasing and decreasing momentum in sprinting through the interpretation of force/time graphs.

Impulse is the time it takes for a force to be applied to an object or body. It is calculated using the equation:

impulse (N s) = force (N) × time (s)

Synoptic link

Impulse graphs correlate to the concept of ground reaction force covered earlier in this section (see page 63).

Impulse can be used to accelerate or decelerate depending on the amount of force applied and for how long.

When sprinting, the negative impulse occurs when the foot is in contact with the ground. This is shown on an impulse graph below the zero line (Figure 32). The positive impulse occurs as the foot takes off from the floor. This is shown above the zero line.

Note that sprinting is specifically identified as an activity in relation to linear motion.

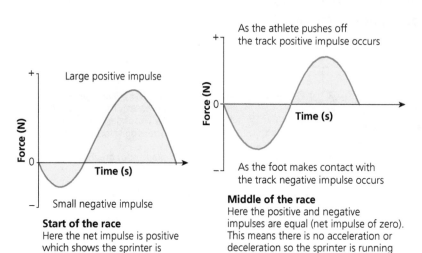
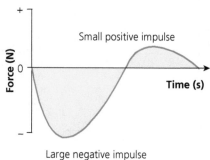

Start of the race
Here the net impulse is positive which shows the sprinter is accelerating

Middle of the race
Here the positive and negative impulses are equal (net impulse of zero). This means there is no acceleration or deceleration so the sprinter is running at a constant velocity

End of the race
Here the net impulse is negative which shows the sprinter decelerating

Figure 32 **Force time graphs to show the relationship between impulse and increasing and decreasing momentum in a 100m sprint**

Do you know?

1 What is meant by the phrase 'centre of mass'?
2 Describe Newton's first law of linear motion.
3 What is meant by the term 'mass'?
4 Which lever operates to allow triceps extension?
5 What is the difference between a scalar and a vector measurement?
6 Describe the impulse created at the start of a sprint race.

4.5 Angular motion

You need to know
- application of Newton's laws to angular motion
- definitions and units for angular motion
- conservation of angular momentum during flight, moment of inertia and its relationship with angular velocity

Angular motion occurs around an axis or fixed point. The force created that turns the body around an axis is called torque.

1st angular law: a rotating body will continue to turn about its axis with a constant torque unless a large enough external force (torque) is exerted upon it. Thus, an ice skater will keep spinning with a constant torque unless a large enough external force is applied.

2nd angular law: the rate of change of angular momentum on a body is proportional to the force (torque) causing it and the change that takes place in the direction in which the force (torque) acts. Thus, if an ice skater tucks up to spin faster, the change in torque will be proportional.

3rd angular law: when a force (torque) is applied by one body on another, the second body will exert an equal and opposite force (torque) on the other body. Thus, if the arms are thrust downwards to complete a seat drop on a trampoline (action), the legs will come up (reaction).

Key terms

Angular motion
Movement which takes place around an axis or fixed point

Torque Turning force

Synoptic link

There are clear similarities between Newton's laws of linear motion and the laws of angular motion.

Definitions and units

You need to know the following definitions, equations and units.

Angular displacement is the smallest change in an angle between the start and finish points of a rotation. It is measured in degrees and radians (1 radian = 57.3 degrees).

Angular velocity is the rotational speed of an object. It refers to the rate of change of angular displacement.

Angular acceleration is the rate of change of angular velocity.

Each can be calculated using the following equations:

$$\text{angular velocity (rad s}^{-1}) = \text{angular displacement (rad)} / \text{time taken (s)}$$

$$\text{angular acceleration (rad s}^{-2}) = \text{change in angular velocity (rad s}^{-1}) / \text{time taken (s)}$$

Conservation of angular momentum

Angular momentum is conserved (constant) unless an external torque (force) acts upon it. The conservation of angular momentum is often shown in a graphical form, showing the relationship between **moment of inertia**, angular momentum and angular velocity.

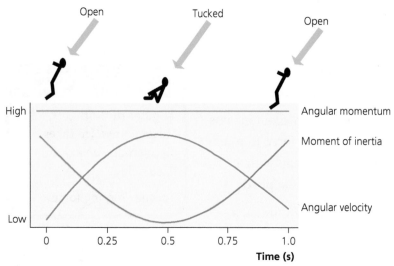

Figure 33 **The stages of a somersault**

The moment of inertia is determined by the distribution of mass from the axis of rotation.

- a large moment of inertia results in a low angular velocity, e.g. tucked somersault (Figure 33)
- a small moment of inertia results in a larger angular velocity, e.g. more open somersault (Figure 33)
- moment of inertia and angular velocity are **inversely proportional**

Do you know?

1 What is meant by the term 'torque'?
2 Describe the moment of inertia during a tucked somersault.
3 Describe the moment of inertia during a more open somersault.
4 What is the relationship between angular velocity and moment of inertia?

4.6 Projectile motion

You need to know
- factors affecting horizontal displacement of projectiles
- factors affecting flight paths of different projectiles
- vector components of parabolic flight

Horizontal displacement

Horizontal displacement is the shortest distance from the starting point to the finishing point. The following factors determine the horizontal displacement of a projectile object, e.g. a shot (Figure 34):
- angle of release (generally, 45° is optimum)
- speed of release (the faster, the better)
- height of release (the higher, the better)

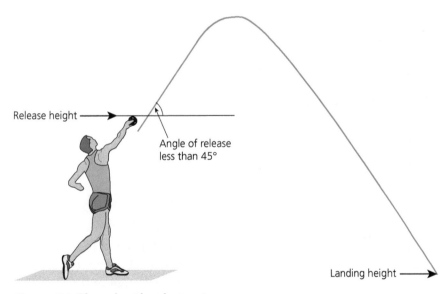

Figure 34 **Throwing the shot put**

Flight paths

A flight path, when drawn as a curve, is known as a **parabola**. The two main factors that affect the parabola of flying projectiles are:
- the weight of the object (gravity)
- the air resistance experienced by the object

Exam tip

Be prepared to suggest the stereotypical flight path (parabola) that would be created for different objects, e.g. shot put, golf ball, football goal kick etc.

Vector components of parabolic flight

Vector components of parabolic flight include a **horizontal component** and a **vertical component**. The vector itself is drawn as an arrow which shows:

- magnitude of force
- direction of force

The bigger the arrow or line of application, the bigger the force created (Figure 35).

Where the horizontal and vertical components are equal, the **resultant vector** shows a line of application which is equally horizontal and vertical (Figure 36).

The **resultant force** is the net direction and magnitude, taking into account the horizontal and vertical components.

Key terms

Horizontal component The horizontal motion of an object

Vertical component The upward motion of an object

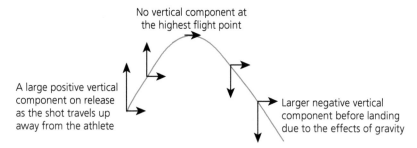

Figure 35 The forces acting on the flight path of a shot put

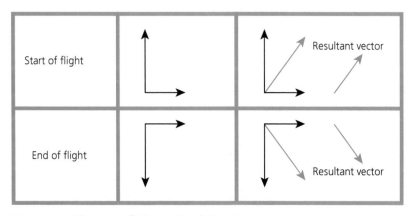

Figure 36 The true flight path of the shot put

Synoptic link

The amount of force created at release relates to the output of the immediate energy store, i.e. the ATP–PC system.

Do you know?

1 What three factors determine the horizontal displacement of an object?
2 What is meant by the term 'parabola'?
3 What two things does a vector show?
4 What is meant by the term 'resultant vector'?

4.7 Fluid mechanics

You need to know
- dynamic fluid force
- factors that reduce and increase drag and their application to sporting situations
- the Bernoulli principle applied to sporting situations

Dynamic fluid force

Fluid dynamics refers to the movement of liquids and gases. **Drag** and lift are dynamic fluid forces.

Drag

- is a force which acts in opposition to motion
- this can be **surface drag** or **form drag**
  - □ surface drag correlates to friction, e.g. the friction created between skin and water when swimming
  - □ form drag relates to streamlining
- if an object is streamlined, the impact of the fluid environment will be minimal
- if you slipstream in cycling, you allow the wind to hit the person in front of you so that the air goes past you with little effect (Figure 37)

The amount of drag is affected by:
- **velocity**, whereby the greater the velocity, the greater the drag
- the **area** of the moving body or object, i.e. the wider the object, the greater the effect of drag

Thus, streamlining helps to reduce drag as the position adopted moves effectively and quickly through the fluid.

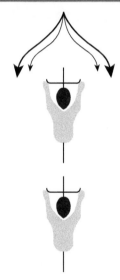

Figure 37 Slipstreaming in cycling

The Bernoulli principle

The Bernoulli principle is concerned with 'lift'. It states that the more lift a sporting object has, the longer and further it will fly.

The angle of release of an object affects how air passes over the top and bottom of an object.

The Bernoulli effect explains how air molecules exert less pressure when they travel faster and more pressure when they travel slower.

For example, if a discus is thrown at the optimal angle (Figure 38):

- air travels quickly above the discus, creating low pressure
- air travels slowly below the discus, creating high pressure
- pressure moves from high to low, causing the discus to lift

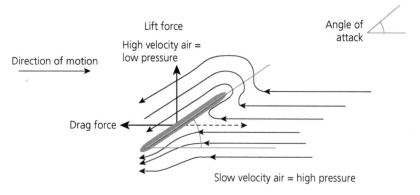

Figure 38 The Bernoulli principle producing a lift force on the discus

The opposite effect can also occur, whereby sports performers want the movement from high to low pressure to push them downwards. This can be created by the body position adopted by speed skiers and cyclists, and by aerodynamic pieces on racing cars, e.g. spoilers.

Exam tips

- The main 'fluid' that the human body travels through relating to drag (notably surface drag) is water, when swimming.
- Note that upward lift force and downward lift force relate particularly to discus, speed skiers, cyclists and racing cars. Simply remember the movement from high to low pressure.

Do you know?

1 What is meant by the term 'fluid dynamics'?
2 Give an example of how streamlining can affect a performance positively.
3 How does the Bernoulli principle explain lift upwards and downwards?
4 When would 'lift' want to be experienced downwards?

Synoptic link

A streamlined position can affect the vector quantity of velocity.

End of section 4 questions

1 What are the exercise-related functions of the different food classes?
2 What are the effects and benefits of a warm up and cool down?
3 State the common types of sporting injury and the ways in which they might be prevented.
4 What are Newton's three laws of linear motion? How are they applied to sporting movements?
5 Name the three classes of lever and describe their use in the body during physical activity and sport.
6 Give an example of the Bernoulli effect in relation to lift upwards and lift downwards?

5 Sport psychology

5.1 Aspects of personality and attitudes

You need to know
- understanding of the nature versus nurture debate in the development of personality (trait and social learning)
- interactionist perspective (Hollander, Lewin)
- how knowledge of interactionist perspective can improve performance
- the Triadic model

Aspects of personality

Nature versus nurture

The nature versus nurture debate involves the concepts that:
- **nature:** personality is wholly inherited
- **nurture:** personality is wholly learned/experienced

Personality is a person's unique psychological make-up. The personality of sports performers clearly varies from person to person. In trying to understand personality, trait theory and social learning theory present differing perspectives.

Trait theory

Trait theory suggests that personality is innate, stable and enduring. Thus, when considering two personality types, the following assumptions are made:

1. Extrovert personalities are likely to show extrovert characteristics, e.g. sociable, active, talkative, outgoing personality type usually associated with team sports players.
2. Introvert personalities are likely to show introvert characteristics, e.g. quite passive, reserved, shy personality type usually associated with individual sports players.

Social learning theory

Social learning theory suggests that behaviour is learned from significant others by socialisation. Behaviour is most likely to be copied if it is reinforced. The key stages of learned behaviour are shown in Figure 39.

> **Key terms**
>
> Trait Inherited characteristic
>
> Social learning Learning from others

> **Exam tip**
>
> Extroverts and introverts are the two main identified personality types and they are often linked to particular sports or physical activities.

Figure 39 **The social learning approach**

Interactionist perspective

The **interactionist perspective** suggests that a person's traits are used and adapted in relation to the situation a person finds themselves in. Thus, behaviour can change and be adapted to the situation.

Kurt Lewin suggested that **B = f (PE)**, or behaviour is a function of personality and the environment. Thus, personality traits are used and adapted to the situation.

Hollander suggested that personality is made up of three features (Figure 40):

■ the core of the performer — 1 (beliefs and values — unlikely to change)
■ the typical responses — 2 (usual responses to situations — may change)
■ the role-related behaviour — 3 (situation-specific behaviour — likely to change)

Knowledge of an interactionist perspective could improve performance in the following ways:

■ coaches may be able to predict behaviour in certain situations
■ action can then be taken to remove the performer or utilise their personality
■ a coach can help a performer to control their behaviour
■ a coach could identify situations that cause specific responses and recreate these in training

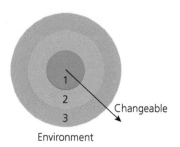

Figure 40 **The Hollander model**

> ### Exam tip
>
> For this topic, you need to be aware of how interactionist perspectives can improve performance.

> ### Synoptic link
>
> Analysis using technology may provide information that suggests a behavioural change is necessary.

Attitudes

Triadic model

An **attitude** is a value or behaviour that is aimed at another attitude, object or thing. The Triadic model suggests that there are three parts or components of an attitude:

■ **cognitive:** what you think and know
■ **affective:** your feelings about the attitude, object or thing
■ **behavioural:** what you do about it

For example:

■ cognitive: I think I should try to be healthy and fit
■ affective: I feel like I should go to the gym
■ behavioural: I go to the gym

> ### Exam tip
>
> Remember the components of an attitude using the acronym 'CAB':
> Cognitive
> Affective
> Behavioural

In this case, attitudes can only be *formed* if a cognitive component exists. For example, if you don't know or think anything about an attitude, object or thing then you can't have an attitude towards it.

There are two main ways to *change* a person's attitude: cognitive dissonance and persuasion.

Cognitive dissonance

A coach may give new information to the performer to cause unease and motivate change. If a person doesn't like something and the coach makes it fun, this new information may challenge their previous attitude. Equally, using a knowledgeable, motivational role model may help to challenge someone's current attitude.

Persuasive communication

This involves new information being given to a person whereby:
- the timing of the message is effective
- the message itself is clear
- the person giving the message is of high status
- the person receiving the message may be willing to accept new information

Synoptic link

A person's attitude can be linked to poor lifestyle choices and the subsequent effects on the respiratory system.

Key terms

Dissonance Creation of conflict

Persuasion Communication to promote change

Do you know?

1 What is the first component of an attitude?
2 How does persuasive communication work?
3 What are the three components of attitude collectively known as?

5.2 Arousal

You need to know
- theories of arousal
- practical applications of theories of arousal and their impact on performance
- characteristics of peak flow experience

Arousal is the level of activation of the reticular activating system, varying from deep sleep to intense excitement. It is a level of readiness and can determine a person's drive to perform.

Key term

Drive Desire or motivation to do something

Theories of arousal

Drive theory

Drive theory suggests that as arousal and motivation increase so does performance (Figure 41). Performance is said to be a function of drive and habit. This is expressed as:

P = f(H × D)

It is too simplistic to suggest that high arousal equals high performance. The explanation of this theory is taken further when looking at dominant response.

Dominant response is the habitual response that is thought to be correct by the performer, even at high arousal levels. This relates closely to the level of the performer:

- **cognitive performers:** dominant response is likely to be undeveloped and of a poor level
- **autonomous performers:** dominant response is developed and of a high level

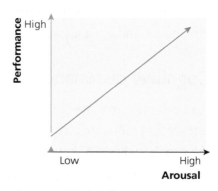

Figure 41 Drive theory

Inverted U theory

This theory suggests that the link between arousal and performance reaches an **optimal point** at moderate levels of arousal (Figure 42).

This can be explained as follows:

- as arousal increases so does performance
- up to an optimal point of arousal
- as arousal increases further, performance decreases

The point of optimal arousal will vary depending on:

- the **characteristics** of the skill (gross skills need more arousal)
- level of **performance** (cognitive performers are often unable to cope with high arousal levels)
- **personality** (extroverts tend to perform more comfortably with high arousal than introverts)

> ### Exam tip
>
> You need to know the practical applications of arousal theories and their potential explanations in relation to performance.

> ### Synoptic link
>
> Arousal can be linked to understanding of the nature vs nurture debate in the development of personality.

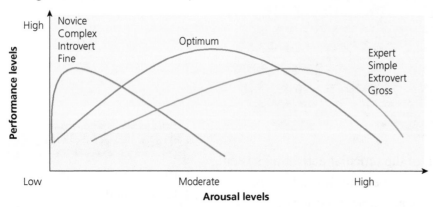

Figure 42 Adaptations to the inverted U theory showing how the task and the performer can affect the optimal level of arousal for best performance

Catastrophe theory

This theory suggests that increased arousal improves performance to an optimal point, but there is a dramatic reduction in performance when arousal increases beyond this optimal point (Figure 43). This dramatic reduction is due to high levels of somatic and cognitive anxiety.

Key terms

Somatic Physiological

Cognitive Psychological

Synoptic link

There are many similarities between the effects of arousal and anxiety.

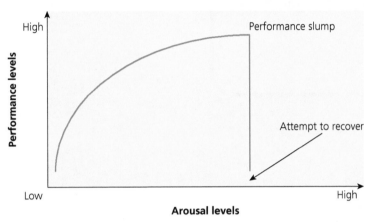

Figure 43 **Catastrophe theory**

Zone of optimal functioning theory

This suggests that rather than having an optimal arousal point, performers have a zone or area when this happens.

Some performers find their zone at low arousal while others experience this at higher arousal (Figure 44).

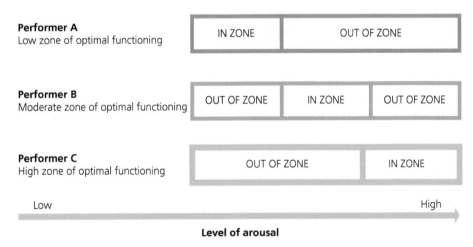

Figure 44 **The zone of optimal functioning**

Peak flow experience

Peak flow experience is when a performer experiences the ultimate intrinsic experience as a result of a positive mental attitude, supreme confidence, focus and efficiency. Their performance appears effortless, fluent and consistent.

However, peak flow will not be experienced if:

- the performer is poorly prepared
- the environment negatively affects the potential to experience peak flow (e.g. referee, crowd, conditions)
- injury, fatigue or concentration loss is experienced

Do you know?

1 What does drive theory suggest?
2 What does inverted U theory suggest?
3 What is a 'dominant response'?

5.3 Anxiety

You need to know

- types of anxiety including somatic, cognitive, competitive trait and competitive state
- advantages and disadvantages of using observations, questionnaires and physiological means to measure anxiety

Anxiety can be defined as a state of nervousness and worry. It can include irrational thinking. There are different types of anxiety:

- **somatic:** a physiological response to a threat, e.g. increased heart rate or 'butterflies in your stomach' (Figure 45)
- **cognitive:** a psychological response, e.g. worrying about losing (Figure 45)
- **competitive trait:** a disposition to suffer from nervousness in most competitive sporting situations
- **competitive state:** a nervous response to specific sporting situations, e.g. being specifically worried about somersaults when trampolining

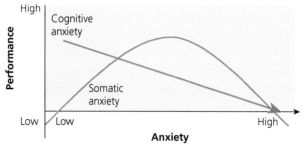

Figure 45 **The relationship between cognitive anxiety, somatic anxiety and performance**

Synoptic link

You can see from Figure 45 that somatic anxiety positively affects performance at a moderate level, similar to the inverted U theory of arousal.

There are three main ways of measuring anxiety in sport:

- **observations:** watching people to gauge their apparent anxiety
- **self-report** questionnaires: e.g. SCAT (sport competition anxiety test) or CSAI2 (competitive sport anxiety inventory)
- **physiological testing:** e.g. monitoring heart rate, respiratory rate, hormone secretion

You will need to be aware of the advantages and disadvantages of each method of measuring anxiety, as outlined in Table 26.

Key term

Questionnaire A set of questions to measure or assess something

Table 26

Method	Advantages	Disadvantages
Observations	■ True to life ■ Easy to conduct	■ Results based on opinion. ■ Observer needs to know the participant to understand the norm. ■ Those observed may feel like they are being watched.
Self-report questionnaires	■ Quick ■ Cheap ■ Used with many performers	■ Performers may lie. ■ Answers depend on mood state. ■ Answers given may be designed to be socially desirable. ■ Can misinterpret question.
Physiological testing	■ Factual ■ Can be measured in different environments, e.g. during games, training etc.	■ Wearing a device could restrict movement. ■ Coaches need to understand the technology. ■ Wearing a device may actually cause anxiety.

Synoptic link

Physiological testing of anxiety can be linked to the use of technology in sport.

Do you know?

1 What is the difference between cognitive and somatic anxiety?
2 What is anxiety about a sports-specific situation called?
3 Name one type of self-report questionnaire for anxiety.

5.4 Aggression

You need to know

- the difference between aggression and assertive behaviour
- theories of aggression, including instinct theory, frustration–aggression hypothesis, social learning theory and aggressive cue theory
- strategies to control aggression

Aggressive and assertive behaviour

Aggressive behaviour is the intent to harm outside the rules, a form of hostility. An example would be deliberately elbowing someone in the face during a game of netball.

Assertive behaviour is well-motivated behaviour, which is within the rules. An example would be tackling someone in football. Tackling is allowed and although someone may get injured, that is not the intention.

There are of course, examples when it is hard to classify whether a sporting act is aggressive or assertive (Figure 46 and Table 27). A boxing punch intends to harm but is within the rules!

Table 27

Aggression	Assertiveness
Intent to harm	Well-motivated
Outside of rules	Within the rules
Hostile	Goal-directed
Deliberate	Controlled
Loss of control	No deliberate intent to harm

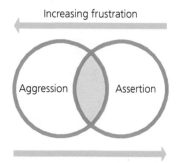

Figure 46 **The overlap between aggression and assertion**

There are many theories to explain why aggression occurs including:
- instinct theory
- frustration–aggression hypothesis
- social learning theory
- aggression cue theory

Instinct theory

Instinct theory suggests that aggression is a result of natural instincts. It proposes that:
- aggression is spontaneous and innate
- aggressive 'animal instincts' surface when faced with threat
- once aggression is released, a cathartic effect is experienced (emotions are expressed and calm is experienced)
- sport can be used to experience catharsis

> ### Key term
> **Catharsis** The release of emotion leading to a calming effect (often due to playing sport)

Frustration–aggression hypothesis

This hypothesis suggests that aggression is inevitable when goals are blocked and the performer becomes frustrated. It proposes that:
- frustration leads to aggression
- the release of aggression can lower the level of frustration

- if aggression is not released or is punished, further frustration can lead to further aggression
- for example, if a footballer is continually prevented from achieving their goal to cross a ball, they may become frustrated and aggressive

Social learning theory

Social learning suggests that aggression is a learned response. It proposes that:
- aggressive acts are observed and copied
- you are more likely to copy an aggressive act if the act is reinforced by others
- aggressive behaviour is more likely to be copied if it is consistent

Synoptic link

Social learning theory is also covered in principles and theories of learning and performance.

Aggression cue theory

The aggression cue theory suggests that aggression is caused by a learning trigger. It proposes that:
- a learned trigger or cue acts as a stimulus to act aggressively
- the cue may come from fellow performers or coaches
- the cue may be another performer or certain equipment, e.g. boxing gloves or enticement by the crowd

Exam tip

For this topic, you need to be aware of the strategies which can be used to control aggression. Remember the four theories of aggression by the sentence: 'I have an **instinct** that my **frustration** is the **cue** to **social learning**.'

Controlling aggression

The following strategies can be employed by coaches, officials and the sport itself:
- punish aggressive behaviour (coaches/officials)
- promote non-aggressive role models (coaches/sport)
- promote assertiveness over aggression (coaches)
- encourage stress-management techniques (coaches)
- provide responsibility (coaches)
- apply the rules fairly and consistently (officials)
- fair-play awards and education campaigns (sport)

Do you know?

1 What is the difference between aggressive and assertive behaviour?
2 What does instinct theory suggest?
3 How can role models be used to prevent aggression?
4 Suggest two strategies that officials can use to prevent aggressive behaviour.

5.5 Motivation and achievement motivation theory

You need to know

- types of motivation
- Atkinson's model of achievement motivation
- characteristics of personality components of achievement motivation
- impact of situational component of achievement motivation
- achievement goal theory
- strategies to develop approach behaviours leading to improvements in performance

Types of motivation

Motivation is seen as the drive to succeed or the desire to achieve something, or to be inspired to do something. There are four types of motivation:

1 **Intrinsic:** the drive from within, such as for pride, satisfaction, a sense of accomplishment or self-worth
2 **Extrinsic:** the drive to perform well or to win in order to gain external rewards such as prizes, trophies or money
3 **Tangible:** real or actual, capable of being touched as it has a physical presence
4 **Intangible**: incapable of being perceived by the sense of touch and not having a physical presence

Achievement motivation

Atkinson's model of achievement motivation relates to how much desire and drive a performer has to persist in trying to succeed. It can be summarised as:

> drive to succeed – fear of failure

A person's motivation and drive to succeed is dependent on which one of two personality types they have (Table 28):

- **NAF:** need to avoid failure
- **NACH:** need to achieve, adopting approach behaviour

Key terms

Achievement motivation
The persistence of a performer to succeed, as a result of desire and drive

Approach behaviour
Showing NACH characteristics to persist towards success

Table 28

Characteristics of NACH	Characteristics of NAF
Approach behaviour	Avoidance behaviour
Task persistence	Dislike feedback
Seek challenges	Take easy option
Take risks	Give up easily
Enjoy evaluation	Lack confidence
Not afraid to fail	Avoid 50/50 challenges
Value feedback	
Attribute success internally	
Confident	
Want to improve, be the best	

The adoption of a NAF or NACH perspective may be situation-specific and depend upon the incentive value and probability of success within the task being completed.

Be aware that a NAF performer strongly fears evaluation and feedback. They may try a task if they do not feel that the evaluation and feedback will be forthcoming.

Synoptic link

Note that this topic is closely linked to the topic of motivation, further developing the content covered. It can also be closely linked to aspects of personality.

Achievement goal theory

Achievement goal theory proposes that the motivation and persistence of a performer is dependent upon the goal set and how success will be measured:

- **task-orientated goals** could relate to technique and personal performance comparisons, so achieving this goal does not depend on the outcome and confidence tends to be maintained
- **outcome-orientated goals** tend to focus on the outcome or result and if this is not achieved then confidence may drop

Developing approach behaviour

Coaches can develop approach behaviour using the following strategies:

- encourage attribution of success to internal factors
- reinforce acceptable behaviour
- encourage and ensure success
- improve self-confidence
- set realistic goals, predominantly task-orientated

Exam tip

For this topic, you need to be aware of the strategies available to develop approach behaviours in order to bring about improvements in performance.

Do you know?

1 What is 'motivation'?
2 What is the difference between something tangible and something intangible?
3 How do NACH and NAF personalities differ?
4 What equation summarises achievement motivation?

5.6 Social facilitation

You need to know

- social facilitation and social inhibition
- evaluation apprehension
- strategies to eliminate the adverse effects of social facilitation and social inhibition

Zajonc's model

Zajonc's model of social facilitation deals with the effect of the presence of others on performance (Figure 47). Other people cause a rise in the performer's arousal levels, which subsequently increases the chance of producing a dominant response.

Two possible outcomes can occur as a result of the influence of those who are present:

- **social facilitation:** the positive effect of the presence of others on performance
- **social inhibition:** the negative effect of the presence of others on performance

> ### Exam tip
>
> You need to be aware of strategies to eliminate the adverse effects of social facilitation and social inhibition.

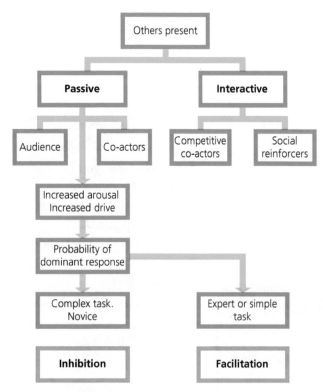

Figure 47 The Zajonc model

The different people who are present can be divided into:
- **social re-enforcers:** for example, supportive coach, family or friends
- **audience:** those simply spectating
- **co-actors:** those doing the same thing, e.g. team mates
- **competitive co-actors:** those acting in direct competition

Evaluation apprehension

Evaluation apprehension refers to the perceived fear of being judged. This can be stronger when a significant other is attending or the person is not confident about the outcome.

Strategies available

Remember that the theory of social facilitation states that social facilitation can have an adverse effect, called social inhibition. Thus, by providing strategies to eliminate the adverse effects of social inhibition, we are in fact giving strategies to eliminate the adverse effects of the social facilitation theory.

The following strategies can be used to eliminate the adverse effects of social inhibition:
- get performers used to an audience
- gradually increase the size of the audience
- gradually introduce evaluation
- aim to improve focus and concentration

Synoptic link

There is a link between evaluation apprehension and selective attention (information processing).

Do you know?

1 What is social facilitation?
2 What is social inhibition?
3 What is evaluation apprehension?

5.7 Group dynamics

You need to know

- group formation
- cohesion
- Steiner's model of potential and actual productivity, faulty group processes
- Ringelmann effect and social loafing
- strategies to improve cohesion, group productivity and overcome social loafing to enhance team performance

Successful teams or groups are not simply individuals; they work cohesively together. Bruce Tuckman suggested five stages of group formation:

1 **Forming:** form and get to know each other
2 **Storming:** personal conflict possible, strive for position or status
3 **Norming:** conflicts have been resolved, standards are accepted
4 **Performing:** group complete their role to achieve group goals
5 **Mourning:** group disband

Cohesion

Cohesion is the tendency for individuals to work together to achieve their goals. This involves the forces that keep the group members on task. This can involve:

- **task cohesion:** individuals working together to achieve a result
- **social cohesion:** individuals relating to each other within the group

It is best if a group has both task and social cohesion. However, task cohesion is generally more important than social cohesion, as task cohesion ensures that the group are working towards their goals and can lead to social cohesion.

Steiner's model of productivity

Steiner suggested that the results of group efforts could be based on an equation that sums up the influence of cohesion:

actual productivity = potential productivity – losses due to faulty processes

Potential productivity is the best performance based on player ability and group resources, **actual productivity** is the actual outcome of group performances, and **faulty group processes** are the things that go wrong to reduce group outcomes and prevent group potential being reached (Figure 48). These can include **motivational losses** and **coordination losses**.

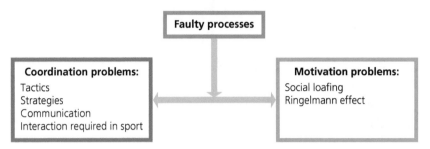

Figure 48 **Summary of faulty processes in group performance**

The Ringelmann effect

The Ringelmann effect suggests that group performance decreases with increased group size. Thus in a tug of war, the bigger the team, the lower the individual effort. This is particularly the case if a performer does not feel valued.

Social loafing

The term **social loafing** is used to identify an individual loss of motivation due to lack of performance identification, i.e. when individuals are not recognised. In a team, if a performer feels undervalued, they may well perform with less motivation.

Strategies available

Table 29

Aim	Strategies
Improving group cohesion	■ establish clearly defined roles and goals ■ acknowledge contributions ■ provide opportunities for success ■ provide social opportunities
Improving group productivity	■ reduce the chances of coordination losses ■ increase skill and fitness levels ■ provide motivational incentives ■ set realistic goals
Overcoming social loafing	■ recognise contributions ■ provide responsibility ■ set realistic goals ■ avoid situations where social loafing could occur

Do you know?

1 Which stage in Tuckman's stages of group formation involves the group initially getting together?
2 Name the two types of cohesion.
3 What is social loafing?

5.8 Importance of goal setting

You need to know

- benefits and types of goal setting, including outcome goals, task-orientated, performance-related and process goals
- principles of effective goal setting

Setting realistic goals has many benefits:

- motivates performers
- improves cohesion
- increases confidence
- prevents social loafing

The different types of goals that can be set are:

- **outcome:** goals set against the performance of others and based on a result
- **task-orientated:** aimed to achieve a better performance level or technique
- **performance-related:** the performer sets a goal to better their own performance rather than comparing themselves to others
- **process:** goals aimed at improving technique only

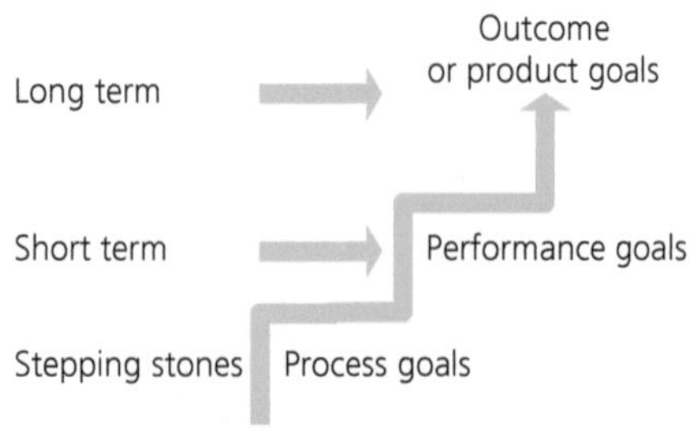

Key terms

Outcome The result

Process How you reach the conclusion/outcome

Goal setting Recording a target to achieve

Synoptic link

Goal setting links to achievement motivation, as a goal will only be achieved if the person welcomes the challenge to achieve it (NACH characteristics).

Figure 49 **Goal-setting summary**

Effective goal setting

Effective goal setting (Figure 49) should include 'SMARTER' principles:

- **specific:** to the muscles used, energy systems used, movements used and the sport itself
- **measurable:** objectively, e.g. distance, time etc.
- **achievable:** should have ability, skill or talent to achieve the goal
- **realistic:** possible for it to be achieved in that time, using resources available within the constraints of the person's life etc.
- **time-bound:** set over a specified period of time
- **evaluate:** should be evaluated regularly to check if it is being met or needs to be adjusted
- **re-do:** goals should be re-set or evaluated during and after completion

Exam tips

- There are several versions of the SMARTER acronym, so be sure to use this specific one.
- Ensure that you could set SMARTER goals for sporting examples.

Do you know?

1 What is an outcome goal?

2 What is a process goal?

3 What does 'SMARTER' stand for?

5.9 Attribution theory

You need to know

- the attribution process linked to Weiner's model and its application to sporting situations
- the link between attribution, task persistence and motivation
- self-serving bias
- attribution retraining
- learned helplessness
- strategies to avoid learned helplessness, leading to improvements in performance

Attribution process

Attributions are the reasons given by a performer for their success or failure. The attributions used can affect a performer's confidence level.

Weiner's model

Weiner suggested that the reasons given for winning and losing (attributions) could be classified as either:

- internal (within their control), or
- external (out of the performer's control)

Examples:

- internal stable attribution, e.g. ability
- internal unstable attribution, e.g. effort
- external stable attribution, e.g. task difficulty
- external unstable attribution, e.g. luck

The premise behind Weiner's model is that stable attributions are unlikely to change in the short term and unstable attributions are likely to change in the short term.

Thus, when success is experienced, internal stable attributions are likely to promote task persistence and motivation.

When defeat is experienced, unstable external factors should be used. This is known as a **self-serving bias** (Figure 50).

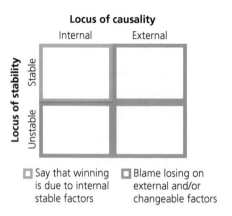

Figure 50 **Weiner's model of attribution showing self-serving bias**

Key term

Self-serving bias
Attributing failure to external unstable factors

Attribution retraining

Attribution retraining involves changing the reasons given for success and failure. A coach who attempts to retrain the attributions of a performer may enhance their confidence (Figure 51).

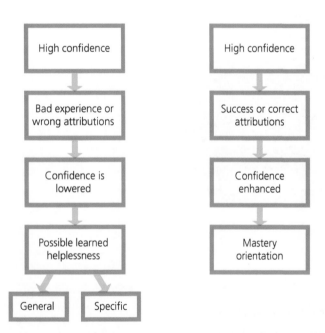

Figure 51 **Confidence can be affected by the attribution process**

Learned helplessness

Learned helplessness is a global or specific belief that failure is inevitable. It often results from using internal stable reasons for losing. Examples include:

- global: I think I will fail at all sports
- specific: I think I will fail at taking this penalty kick

Strategies to prevent learned helplessness include:

- attribution retraining: learning from a coach to change attributions for failure into external unstable reasons, and attributions for success into internal stable reasons
- allow early success to develop confidence
- set realistic goals
- point out previous successes
- use of stress management techniques

Exam tip

For this topic, you need to be aware of possible strategies to avoid learned helplessness, which would lead to improvements in performance.

Synoptic link

The topics of learned helplessness and attribution retraining link closely to that of confidence.

Do you know?

1 What term is used to explain the reasons given for success or failure?
2 Give an example of an internal stable attribution.
3 Self-serving bias would result in what attribution being used for failure?
4 What is learned helplessness?

5.10 Self-efficacy and confidence

You need to know

- characteristics of self-efficacy, self-confidence and self-esteem
- Bandura's model of self-efficacy
- Vealey's model of self-confidence
- effects of home field advantage
- strategies to develop high levels of self-efficacy, leading to improvements in performance

Bandura's model

Bandura suggests that **self-efficacy** varies with the situation and is affected by four factors:

- **performance accomplishments:** have you done it before?
- **vicarious experiences:** watching a model of similar ability
- **verbal persuasion:** encouragement from others
- **emotional arousal:** a perception of the effects of anxiety on performance

Self-efficacy can increase motivation and approach behaviour and can ultimately improve performance (Figure 52).

Key terms

Self-efficacy A belief in one's ability to master a specific sporting situation

Self-confidence A belief in one's self and one's ability to complete tasks

Self-esteem Respect for one's self; can occur as a result of increased confidence

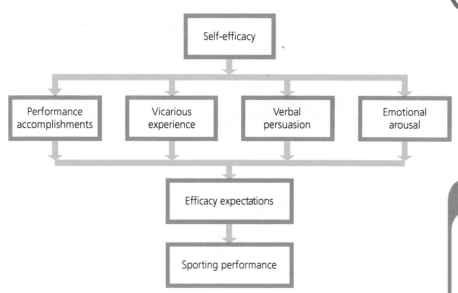

Figure 52 **Strategies to improve self-efficacy**

Exam tip

For this topic, you should concentrate on considering strategies to develop high levels of self-efficacy, which lead to improvements in performance.

Vealey's model

Vealey suggests that **self-confidence** is affected by the interaction of factors, including:

- **trait confidence:** a belief that you can do well in a range of sports
- **state confidence:** a belief that you can do well in a specific sport or moment
- the **situation** performers are in
- **competitive orientation:** the degree to which performers are drawn towards competitive scenarios

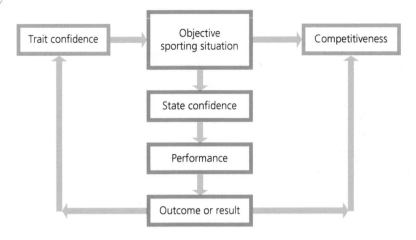

Figure 53 Vealey's model of sports confidence

A person with a high trait confidence and competitive orientation is likely to believe that they can succeed in a situation, showing state confidence. Ultimately, they will evaluate their performance, which will affect the next time they face a similar situation (Figure 53).

Home-field advantage

When playing at a home venue, the crowd can have a positive or negative effect on performers. The balance between confidence and anxiety is a key factor.

If the crowd is supportive and confidence is high, anxiety will be low and a home-field advantage is experienced. The 'away' team may feel anxious.

If the crowd is hostile towards the 'home' team, confidence will be low and anxiety will be high, thus there is no home-field advantage. The 'away' team may feel more confident.

> ## Key term
>
> **Home-field advantage**
> A balance of confidence and anxiety whereby the home crowd provide an advantage for the home team

> ## Synoptic link
>
> Confidence is closely linked to goal setting and attribution theory, as a performer must be confident they can achieve their goal and attribute failure to external unstable factors.

Do you know?

1 What is the difference between self-efficacy and self-confidence?
2 What is trait confidence?
3 What is state confidence?
4 Does a large 'home' crowd definitely help the home team?

5.11 Leadership

You need to know

- characteristics and styles of effective leaders
- evaluation of leadership styles for different sporting situations
- prescribed and emergent leaders
- theories of leadership in different sporting situations

Characteristics of effective leaders

A leader has followers. The common characteristics of effective leaders include:

- charisma
- good communication skills
- knowledgeable
- motivational
- empathy
- experience

You should be aware of two types of leader:

- **prescribed:** appointed from outside the group, often by a set board of people
- **emergent:** appointed or emerging naturally from within the group

Key term

Leader Someone who has influence in helping others to achieve their goals

Styles of leadership

Different styles of leadership can be used effectively in different sporting situations.

Kurt Lewin proposed three main styles of leadership:

Autocratic

- a leader who makes the decisions without consulting with the group
- can be perceived as bossy and overpowering
- could be effective when coach has to change tactics, substitute a player or discipline a performer

Democratic

- decisions are made with group consultation
- can take time
- senior team members may get their say on decisions or a coach may welcome the opinion of the whole team

Exam tip

For this topic, you need to be aware of the possible leadership style which would be most appropriate in a particular sporting scenario.

Laissez-faire

- the leader does very little and leaves the group to it
- when the group is performing, it is sometimes better to simply let them play with little to no involvement from the coach
- however, this level of performance might not continue without intervention

Theories of leadership

Fiedler's contingency theory

This looks at how favourable a situation is and suggests the style of leadership which should then be used (Figure 54). The styles proposed are:

- **task-orientated:** autocratic to get the task done
- **person-orientated:** democratic to work on relationships

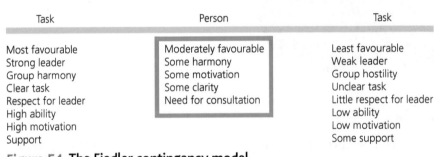

Task	Person	Task
Most favourable	Moderately favourable	Least favourable
Strong leader	Some harmony	Weak leader
Group harmony	Some motivation	Group hostility
Clear task	Some clarity	Unclear task
Respect for leader	Need for consultation	Little respect for leader
High ability		Low ability
High motivation		Low motivation
Support		Some support

Figure 54 **The Fiedler contingency model**

Chelladurai's multi-dimensional model

Chelladurai acknowledges that leadership style is chosen as a result of multi-dimensional factors, not just the situation. These include behaving in a manner which consists of a mixture of the required behaviour and preferred behaviour (Figure 55).

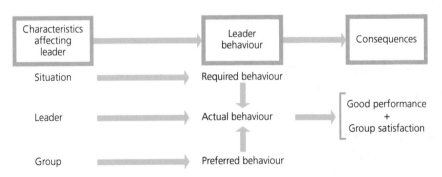

Figure 55 **The Chelladurai model of leadership**

Synoptic link

Fiedler's theory and Chelladurai's model link to the concept of group cohesion, as an effective leader can facilitate cohesion within a group.

Exam tip

Read Chelladurai's model from right to left: to achieve quality performance and satisfaction, the leader needs to behave with a mixture of required and preferred behaviour while taking the situation and their own and the group's characteristics into account.

5.12 Stress management

You need to know

- explanation of the terms 'stress' and 'stressor'
- use of warm up for stress management
- effects and explanation of cognitive and somatic techniques on the performer

Stress and stressors

Any form of **stressor** can cause **stress**. If a performer experiences stress (e.g. as a result of injury, the opposition, the officials, the result), varying techniques can be used to reduce stress. These are called stress-management techniques.

Stress-management techniques

The following techniques can be incorporated into a warm up as a means of controlling stress:

Somatic techniques

- **biofeedback:** making use of a measuring device to help the performer recognise the physical changes that will happen under stress, e.g. change in heart rate
- **breathing control:** exaggerated deep breaths
- **centering:** a form of breathing control to help relax performers, focusing on breathing and relaxing the shoulders and abdomen
- **progressive muscle relaxation:** where muscles are tensed and then released slowly while breathing deeply

Key terms

Stressor Anything that leads to an anxious state

Stress A negative response of the body to a threat, causing anxiety

Cognitive techniques

- **psychological skills training (PST):** training and practising any of the methods used as cognitive stress-management techniques, often led by a sports psychiatrist
- **mental rehearsal, visualisation and imagery:** cognitive relaxation techniques involving the control of mental thoughts and imagining positive outcomes
- **attentional control and cue utilisation:** the ability to choose an attention style which allows the performer to process and focus on key information/cues
- **thought stopping:** a learned action or trigger to remove negative and irrational thoughts
- **positive self-talk:** developing cognitive positive thoughts about your own performance

Do you know?

1 What is stress caused by?
2 How do cognitive and somatic stress differ?
3 What is mental rehearsal?

End of section 5 questions

1 How does the interactionist theory suggest that behaviour is more than simply a result of personality?
2 What effects can arousal and anxiety can have on a performance?
3 What does achievement motivation theory consist of?
4 What are Tuckman's stages of group formation?
5 List some benefits of goal setting.
6 How can stress can be managed?

Synoptic links

Stress management techniques link closely with the earlier topics of arousal and anxiety. They also link with Section 4 and warm ups.

Attentional control has a direct link to arousal and anxiety.

Exam tip

There is no single tried and tested method of stress management that works for everyone. Simply ensure you have an overview of each technique.

6 Sport and society and the role of technology

6.1 Concepts of physical activity and sport

You need to know
- characteristics and functions of key concepts, including physical recreation, sport, physical education and school sport
- comparison of the characteristics of key concepts

Physical recreation

Physical recreation is the active part of a person's leisure or free time. The person has voluntarily chosen to participate in activities, without necessarily focusing on winning. It may simply be to 'take part' and to enjoy oneself. Physical recreation has these key characteristics:

- fun
- non-serious
- effort is applied
- flexible in nature
- often self-officiated
- participation is a choice

Physical recreation serves many functions:
- develops self-confidence
- releases stress
- develops skills
- enhances social skills
- provides fun
- improves health, thereby reducing strain on the NHS
- develops social control of society
- increases social integration and community cohesion

Sport

Sport is deemed as serious activity that is competitive in nature. There are a number of key characteristics which describe sport:

- structured
- competitive
- uses strategies and tactics
- rewards often available
- set rules
- uses specialist equipment
- high skill levels
- serious in nature

Many of the benefits of physical recreation are also applicable to sport, but some additional benefits of sport include:

- provides social opportunities
- develops positive attitudes
- increases social integration between different socio-economic and ethnic groups
- creates employment opportunities (e.g. coaches, lifeguards etc.)

Physical education

Physical education (PE) is a curriculum-based programme of education to develop health and fitness. The National Curriculum was launched in 1988 and developed a set programme for educators to teach to schoolchildren (Figure 56). PE has many distinctive characteristics:

- participation is compulsory
- formally taught in lessons
- begins in primary school
- lessons are planned and structured into key stages
- takes place during school time

Physical education promotes a positive attitude towards exercise. Physical skills are developed but opportunities are also promoted in aspects of leadership, personal and social skills, and communication.

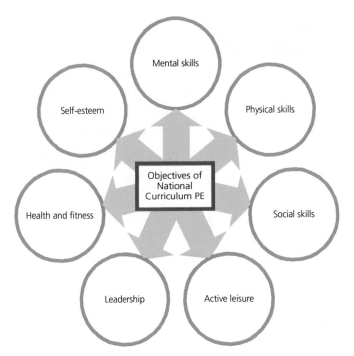

Figure 56 The objectives of the National Curriculum for PE

School sport

School sport generally occurs in extra-curricular time and is optional for children to attend.

School sport includes the generic benefits of sport (see above) while linking the skills learned from physical education to a more competitive environment. This may involve representing the school and competing against other schools. It can also include the use of sports coaches.

Concept comparison

Table 30

	Physical recreation	Sport	Physical education	School sport
Who for?	Available to all	For those good enough to be selected	All pupils	For the chosen few/ those who choose to attend
When?	In free time	At set times	In timetabled PE lessons	Extra-curricular time
Structure	Can be structured but does not have to be	Structured, with rules etc.	Structured/planned	Structured/planned
Fitness level required	Varied	Usually at a higher level	Varied	Usually at a higher level
Compulsory?	No, voluntary/optional	No, voluntary/ optional unless a career	Yes	No

Do you know?

1 Which of the following are compulsory?
   ■ physical recreation
   ■ sport
   ■ physical education
   ■ school sport
2 Name two major benefits of a physical education programme.
3 Is sport structured or unstructured?
4 When is physical recreation undertaken?
5 When is school sport completed?

6.2 Development of elite performers

You need to know

- the personal, social and cultural factors required to support progression from talent identification to elite performance
- the generic roles, purpose and the relationship between organisations in providing support and progression from talent identification through to elite performance. This includes national governing bodies, national institutes of sport and UK sport
- the key features of national governing bodies' whole sport plans
- the support services provided by national institutes of sport for talent development
- the key features of UK Sport's World Class Performance Programme, Gold Event Series and Talent Identification and Development

Personal, social and cultural factors

There are many personal, social and cultural factors which affect how smoothly a performer can progress from being identified as a talent to elite performance level.

Personal factors include:
- goal-orientated
- good communicator, willing to accept and give advice
- focused
- patient
- persistent (in the face of failure)
- determined
- self-confident

Social and cultural factors include:
- socio-economic status (can afford to take part, train etc.)
- structured levels of competition within the sport
- media coverage and access to role models to aspire to
- taking part in a sport which welcomes all genders, sexual orientations, beliefs etc.
- support network of family and friends
- links between education providers and clubs

Key terms

Personal factors The influence of characteristics ingrained within a person

Social factors The influence of those involved in a person's day-to-day life

Cultural factors The influence of variables ingrained in society and a country

Talent Having the potential for world class success, identified through multi-disciplinary screening of athletes

Elite The best, highest-level sports performers

Synoptic link

Media coverage links to the concept of the golden triangle (the interrelationship between sport, business and the media).

Support and provision

The development of performers is heavily influenced by the varying bodies that facilitate a performer's transition to elite level (Table 31). These organisations include UK Sport, national institutes of sport and national governing bodies (NGBs).

Table 31 Objectives and functions of UK Sport, national institutes and NGBs

UK Sport	National institutes of sport (e.g. EIS)	National governing bodies (NGBs)

■ develops high-performance sport in the UK
■ aims to increase sporting excellence
■ invests and distributes lottery money
■ provides funding to NGBs
■ funds athletes directly via Athlete Personal Award
■ provides funding for national institutes of sport, e.g. English Institute of Sport (EIS) and British Olympic and Paralympic programmes
■ runs talent-identification programmes
■ provides personal lifestyle advice
■ develops and manages the UK's international sporting relationships
	The English Institute of Sport (EIS) is a subsidiary of UK Sport which receives a grant every year. The EIS:
	■ provides help and support to NGBs (see below)
	■ provides practitioners to help coaches and performance directors to improve the performance of their athletes
	■ delivers services which enable coaches and performance directors to
	  □ optimise training programmes
	  □ maximise performance in competitions and improve the health and wellbeing of their performers
	■ is the country's largest provider of sport science, medicine, technology and lifestyle support
	■ provides varying 'value-added' benefits to the sports with which it liaises, including world class performance environments and access to cutting edge innovation and research
	■ operates many 'high-performance centres' and 'partner sites', e.g. Team GB rehabilitation unit at Bisham Abbey. These are high-quality facilities with high-quality staff
		NGBs are organisations which have responsibility for managing their own particular sport. NGBs:
		■ promote participation and help to develop elite performers
		■ work with other agencies (e.g. UK Sport and national institutes of sport) to provide a coordinated approach
		■ use positive role models to promote sport and encourage opportunities for all
		■ help to provide accessible facilities for all members of society
		■ aim to meet government-driven policies, e.g. through Whole Sport Plans
		■ put policies in place to target minority or under-represented groups
		■ invest money in deprived inner-city areas
		■ issue Whole Sport Plans (see below)

Whole sport plans

Whole sport plans are documents (like a business plan) which are submitted to Sport England, outlining how an NGB plans to develop participation and talent. These may include how talent will be spotted, nurtured and developed in that sport.

The four-year period for a Whole School Plan is related to this. Between 2013 and 2017, £83 million was allocated to develop young athletes in England.

Talent development

One way in which the EIS, UK Sport and NGBs work together is through a coordinated programme of talent identification.

Talent-identification programmes are designed to screen performers so that they can be directed to the most suitable sport. There is no guarantee of success, but large levels of funding are required to develop those selected. Talent-identification schemes have common key characteristics:

- high-standard testing facilities
- make use of appropriate tests
- keep a database of results
- use widespread testing to ensure equal opportunities
- use high-quality coaches to develop those selected
- plan a clear development pathway

The EIS has a Performance Pathways Team which coordinates an approach with UK Sport to identify and develop talent as part of the World Class Programme. The Pathway programme provides targeted support to nurture and develop talent in the following ways:

- **frontline technical solutions:** meeting sport-specific needs to identify and develop talent
- **education:** developing coaches
- **analytics:** providing meaningful, objective measurements of how well the pathway is working
- **pathway health checks (PHCs):** reviewing systems which develop potential medal winners
- **strategy:** providing distinctive progression pathways

World Class Performance Programme

The key features of UK Sport's World Class Performance Programme (WCPP) are outlined below:

- for those athletes selected, the WCPP provides a structured route to success
- for summer and winter Olympic and Paralympic athletes
- there are two distinctive WCPP levels:
  1 **podium:** financial support for athletes with realistic medal potential at the next Olympic Games
  2 **podium potential:** financial support for athletes with realistic medal potential at the subsequent Olympics, i.e. 8 years away
- there is a talent level below podium potential for athletes who could progress to the two levels of the WCPP

Key terms

Talent identification
Multi-disciplinary screening of athletes in order to identify those with the potential for world class success

Performance Pathways Team A combination of EIS and UK Sport expertise used to identify and develop world class talent

Synoptic link

Performance analytics links to the topic of understanding technology for sports analytics.

Exam tip

The levels of the WCPP may change in time. Stay up to date with any changes.

Gold Event Series

The key features of UK Sport's Gold Event Series are:
- UK Sport's flagship programme
- aims to bring major international events to the UK
- works with the sport(s) and host location in the provision of a business plan and financial support (if the bid is successful)
- works with relevant NGBs

Do you know?

1 Does a performer require personal, social and/or cultural factors to be in place to develop to elite level?
2 What is UK Sport responsible for?
3 Give one example of a national institute of sport.
4 What are NGBs responsible for?
5 Give three characteristics of an effective talent-identification programme.

Exam tip

For this topic, it is advisable to be aware of current, updated, named programmes in addition to those noted here, e.g. UK Sport's World Class Performance Programme. Carry out your own research to find out more about the programmes mentioned here, and about more current and recent ones.

6.3 Ethics in sport

You need to know
- amateurism, the Olympic Oath, sportsmanship, gamesmanship, win ethic
- positive and negative forms of deviance in relation to the performer

Key concepts

Amateurism

- participation in sport for the love of it, receiving no financial gain
- based on the concept of athleticism, being physical endeavour with moral integrity
- still evident in modern-day sport through fair play and sportsmanship.

Key term

Ethics A system of moral principles

Olympic Oath

The Olympic Oath is the promise made by each participant in the Olympic Games:

In the name of all competitors I promise that we shall take part in these Olympic Games, respecting and abiding by the rules which govern them, committing ourselves to a sport without doping and without drugs.

- relevant to promote fair play and sportsmanship at the Olympics
- unfortunately, not followed by all athletes as many examples exist of drug scandals, cheating etc.

Sportsmanship

- conforming to the rules, spirit and etiquette of a sport
- involves high levels of etiquette, e.g. kicking a ball out of play when a football player is injured
- encouraged through NGB campaigns
- encouraged through fair-play awards
- positive role models are used to promote sportsmanship
- promoted by punishing behaviour which is not 'sporting', e.g. anything outside of the rules

Gamesmanship

- bending the rules (without breaking them) and stretching them to their absolute limit without getting caught
- using whatever 'dubious' methods possible to achieve the desired result, e.g. time wasting/moving slowly when a team are ahead or 'sledging' an opponent in cricket

Win ethic

- links to 'winning at all costs'
- outcome is all that matters and finishing second is not an acceptable option
- sometimes known as the Lombardian ethic

Deviance

Positive deviance is behaviour which is outside the norms of society but with no intent to harm or break the rules. It involves over-adherence to the norms or expectations of society, e.g. overtraining or continuing to play when injured.

Negative deviance is behaviour that goes against the norms and has a detrimental effect on individuals and on society in general. The performer is motivated to win at all costs, e.g. by cheating and illegal drug-taking.

Key terms

Etiquette A convention or rule in an activity which is not enforceable, but is usually observed

Lombardian ethic A desire to win at all costs

Exam tip

You should be able to find several current examples of sportsmanship and good etiquette from watching and observing top-level sporting encounters. Conversely, there will also be examples of gamesmanship.

Synoptic link

As a performer sets goals (outcome or task), their motivation to achieve these goals may result in a 'win at all costs'/'Lombardian ethic' and the use of gamesmanship.

6.4 Violence in sport

You need to know

■ the causes and implications of violence in sport in relation to the performer, spectator and sport
■ strategies for preventing violence within sport to the performer and spectator

Causes of violence

The causes of violence in sport vary for the spectator, the performer and the sport (Table 32). Some sports are 'naturally' more violent and aggressive than others. Ice hockey, for example, has relatively frequent fights between players. Football is renowned for spectator violence (hooliganism).

Table 32 **Causes of violence in sport**

Among performers	Among spectators
■ Win-at-all-costs attitude	■ Hype about the event
■ Frustration at performers/referee	■ Poor segregation of fans
■ Retaliation	■ Rivalry
■ Pressure from coaches/sponsors	■ Alcohol/drugs
■ Side-effects of drugs	■ Display of masculinity

Preventing violence

Regarding the performer

Strategies that can help prevent violence include:
■ use of the television match official (TMO) or an additional official
■ retrospective action, whereby at the conclusion of the match/event, footage can be watched and violent behaviour punished
■ 'sin bins', where performers are temporarily excluded for breaching the rules, e.g. the 10-minute yellow card in rugby union
■ performers can be banned for violent behaviour
■ promotion of positive role models
■ fair play and educational campaigns to promote positive behaviour

Key terms

Violence in sport Physical acts committed to harm others in sports such as American football, rugby, football and ice hockey

Hooliganism Acts of vandalism and violence in public places

Regarding spectators

Strategies that can help to prevent violence from spectators include:

- ban or control alcohol consumption
- impose banning orders on spectators
- prevent spectators from travelling
- removal of passports
- CCTV and security measures
- early kick-off times
- laws preventing encroachment onto the field

Synoptic link

There is a clear link between the concept of hooliganism and social control.

Do you know?

1 Name one strategy to prevent violence within sport (in relation to the performer).
2 Name an example of a sport which is deemed to be 'naturally aggressive'.
3 Media hype, rivalry and alcohol are all contributing factors to what?

6.5 Drugs in sport

You need to know

- the social and psychological reasons behind elite performers using illegal drugs and doping methods to aid performance
- the physiological effects of drugs on the performer and their performance, including erythropoietin (EPO), anabolic steroids and beta-blockers
- the positive and negative implications to the sport and the performer of drug-taking
- strategies for elimination of performance-enhancing drugs in sport
- arguments for/against drug-taking and testing

Reasons for drug use

Illegal drugs and doping methods to enhance performance are a major cause of concern in the world of sport. Social reasons behind elite performers using illegal drugs and doping methods to include:

- a 'win-at-all-costs' attitude
- a desire for a level playing field, e.g. 'everyone else is taking them'
- pressure from coaches and sponsors
- poor role models
- poor methods of testing and insignificant punishments

Key term

Doping In competitive sports, doping refers to the use of banned performance-enhancing drugs by athletic performers

Psychological reasons for performers taking these drugs include:

- to steady nerves
- to increase confidence
- to increase aggression

Physiological effects

Table 33 Physiological effects of drugs on the performer

Method of enhancement	What are they?	Reasons why this method is used (i.e. benefits)	Which athletes might use them?	Side-effects
Anabolic steroids	Artificially produced male hormones that mimic testosterone, e.g. THG.	They aid in the storage of protein and promote muscle growth and development of muscle tissue in the body, leading to increased strength and power. They also lead to less fat in the muscle; a lean body weight. They can improve the body's capacity to train for longer at a higher intensity and decrease fatigue associated with training.	They are particularly beneficial to power athletes such as sprinters.	Liver damage, heart and immune system problems, acne, behaviour changes such as aggression, paranoia and mood swings.
Beta-blockers	Help to calm down an individual and decrease anxiety by counteracting the adrenaline that interferes with performance, by preventing it from binding to nerve receptors.	They can be used to improve accuracy in precision sports through steadying the nerves. They calm performance anxiety and aid performance by keeping the heart rate low and decreasing the tremble in the hands. They work by widening the arteries, allowing increased blood flow and reducing involuntary muscle spasms.	Particularly relevant in high-precision sports such as archery, snooker and golf.	Tiredness due to low blood pressure and slower heart rate, which will affect aerobic capacity.
Erythropoietin (EPO)	A natural peptide hormone produced by the kidneys to increase red blood cells. Now it can be artificially manufactured to cause an increase in haemoglobin levels.	It stimulates red blood cell production which leads to an increase in the oxygen-carrying capacity of the body. This can result in an increase in the amount of work performed. It therefore increases endurance and delays the onset of fatigue. An athlete can keep going for longer and recover more quickly from training.	Tends to be used by endurance performers (e.g. long-distance runners and cyclists) who need effective oxygen transport in order to succeed in their sport.	Can result in blood clotting, strokes and, in rare cases, death.

Implications of drug use

It is immoral to argue that there are any positive implications, as such, of illegal performance-enhancing drugs. Some may be able to argue that the enhanced performance levels are worth the risk; however, the negatives to the performer and the sport are compelling (Table 34).

Table 34

	The performer	The sport
Positives	■ enhanced performance (illegally) ■ enhanced confidence/focus/ physiology ■ potential for fame and fortune	■ higher performance levels (however, through illegal means)
Negatives	■ health problems (current and future) ■ reputational damage ■ loss of sponsorship ■ side effects of the drugs ■ bans/fines ■ inability to get further support/sponsorship	■ threatens integrity of sport ■ reputational damage ■ sport becomes associated with drug-taking ■ produces negative role models

Elimination strategies

Sporting authorities are constantly under pressure to take steps to eliminate illegal performance-enhancing drugs.

- UK Anti-Doping (UKAD) is responsible for drug-testing in the UK
- UKAD try to educate athletes on the dangers of drug-taking
- the '100% Me' campaign is delivered to athletes
- UKAD have a coordinated approach with WADA (World Anti-Doping Agency)
- random testing and 'competition testing' takes place
- punishments are intended to be harsh and preventative

Unfortunately, drug cheats are often a step ahead of the testers and find ways to mask (hide) the drugs in their bodies. Drugs are occasionally taken accidentally and there is a lack of consistency in the drug-testing measures from country to country.

Arguments

There are many arguments for and against the use of illegal performance drugs and the process of testing (Tables 35 and 36).

Table 35

For performance-enhancing drugs	Against performance-enhancing drugs
It is an athlete's choice	Immoral
Can help an athlete to recover more quickly	Cheating
Achieves a higher standard of performance	Not 'natural' performance
Sometimes taken for medical reasons	Health implications
Creates a level playing field (if everyone takes them)	Creates negative role models
	Against the Olympic ideal

> **Exam tip**
>
> Methods of testing for performance-enhancing drugs will not be examined.

> **Exam tip**
>
> This topic is frequently in the media as most major sporting events are marred by drug-taking scandals, so keeping up to date is imperative.

Table 36

For drug-testing	Against drug-testing
It is illegal to take such drugs	Expensive
Cheats should not be allowed to compete	Sometimes struggles to keep up with with drug cheats
Prevents unfair advantages	Varies from country to country
Increases integrity of the sport	Doesn't monitor/test all drugs
Spectators can watch a fair competition	Results can be flawed

Synoptic link

There is a link between drug-testing and technology in sport, as the technology used to test for drugs is constantly evolving.

Do you know?

1 What is the main effect of taking beta-blockers?
2 Give one argument against drug-testing.
3 What do UKAD and WADA stand for?

6.6 Sport and the law

You need to know

■ the uses of sports legislation in relation to performers (contracts, injury, loss of earnings), officials (negligence), coaches (duty of care) and spectators (safety, hooliganism)

Law and legislation

Everyone involved in sport is accountable for his or her behaviour. The uses of sports legislation vary between performers, coaches, officials and spectators.

There is a difference between sports law and sports legislation:
■ **sports law** refers to the laws, regulations and judicial decisions that govern sports and athletes who perform in them
■ **sports legislation** refers to laws that are made, or enacted, which relate to sports in particular

Synoptic link

There is a link between violence in sport and sports legislation, in that violence by players or spectators can be punishable in a court of law.

Table 37 shows how the law affects participants and spectators.

Table 37

Performers	■ have contracts with sponsors and employers/clubs which outline acceptable behaviour ■ the 'Bosman Ruling' gives professional footballers in the EU the right to move freely between clubs ■ injury caused by another performer's illegal or violent conduct can result in civil claims being heard in a court of law ■ players can be prosecuted for violent behaviour, which can result in loss of earnings
Officials	■ officials can be seen to be negligent if they allow play on an unsafe surface or for not maintaining safe play ■ if an official's conduct falls below a 'reasonable-person standard' and leads to a breach of their duty of care, resulting in foreseeable harm to another, they can face legal action
Coaches	■ have a duty of care to their performers ■ can be prosecuted for providing/administering illegal performance-enhancing drugs
Spectators	■ can be prosecuted for hooliganism ■ can face bans from travelling to other countries ■ the Football Offences Act (1991) and the Football Spectators Act (1989) help to control spectators

Key term

Duty of care A legal obligation imposed on someone if they are responsible for a group of people

Exam tip

Do not worry about learning all the names of the laws which affect those involved in sport. Rather, summarise the intentions behind these laws.

Do you know?

1 What is the difference between sports law and sports legislation?
2 If an official is seen to be allowing play on an unsafe surface or not maintaining safe play, what is this called?
3 What is the Bosman Ruling?

6.7 Impact of commercialisation and the media

You need to know

■ the positive and negative impact of commercialisation, sponsorship and the media on the performer, the coach, the official, the audience and the sport

Synoptic link

There are links between Section 3 and commercialisation.

The golden triangle

The relationship between business, sport and the media is inter-dependent, i.e. they rely on each other. This relationship is known as the golden triangle (see page 45 in Section 3.)

- the inter-dependent link includes aspects of commercialised activity such as sponsorship and the media
- sponsorship is the provision of money and/or support in exchange for commercial return
- the media is an organised means of communication designed to reach a large audience. It includes television, radio, newspapers, internet and social media

The positive and negative impacts of commercialisation on sport and performers are summarised in Tables 38–40.

> ### Key term
>
> **Commercialisation**
> The treating of sport as a commodity, involving the buying and selling of assets, with the market as the driving force behind sport

Table 38 **Advantages and disadvantages of media coverage for a sport**

Advantages of media coverage	Disadvantages of media coverage
Increase the profile of the sport and individual performers within the sport.	National governing bodies/sports performers lose control to television/sponsors. The traditional nature of a sport is lost; e.g. rule structures/timings of a sport are adapted to suit the demands of television or sponsors.
Increased participation levels within a sport as a result of television coverage which encourages others to take it up (e.g. cycling as a result of Tour de France or football as a result of World Cup coverage).	The media control the location of events, as well as kick-off times and, in some cases, playing seasons (e.g. Super League Rugby switched to a 'summer' game). There is sometimes too much sport on television which can lead to boredom of spectators and/or lower attendance at televised events.
More variations of a sport are developed to make it more 'media friendly', leading to more matches/fixtures for fans to watch (e.g. Twenty20 cricket).	There are inequalities of coverage — more popular sports such as football gain at the expense of minority sports such as squash. Certain prestigious events are now available only on satellite television which requires a subscription payment, e.g. test cricket, golf's Ryder Cup etc. This means there are fewer viewers for some sports due to the increasing control of Sky and BT Sport.
It generates greater income and makes a sport more appealing to sponsors. It increases commercial opportunities, which further increase the financial gain of a sport or performers (e.g. golf, tennis, football).	Demands of media and sponsors negatively impact on high level performers (e.g. demands for interviews, personal appearances etc.).
Increased standards in performance as well as behaviour as a result of an increased media focus.	The media can over-sensationalise certain negative events in sport. A win-at-all-costs attitude develops due to high rewards on offer, which leads to negative, deviant acts and players becoming poor role models (e.g. in football arguing with officials).
Rule changes lead to a speeding up of action/more excitement/entertainment in a sport (e.g. penalty shoot-outs).	More breaks in play (e.g. for adverts) can disrupt the spectator experience.

Table 39 **Positive and negative effects of sponsorship and commercial deals for elite sports performers**

Positives	Negatives
Increased wages, prize money and extrinsic rewards.	Increased pressure to win and a win-at-all-costs attitude to maintain high-level prize money, sponsorship deals etc.
Increased availability of professional contracts where performers are able to devote themselves full time to sport, training harder and longer to improve performance.	An increase in 'deviant' behaviour due to increased pressure to win (e.g. performing when injured or over-training; taking illegal drugs; off-field drinking and gambling).
Performers are increasingly in the public eye and increasingly well known so they need to maintain discipline and behave appropriately to protect a positive image (e.g. on-field via fair play and sportsmanship; off-field via community and charitable work).	Performers are treated as commodities, bought and sold for economic reasons; sponsors become too demanding (e.g. via the requirement to make personal appearances at sponsorship events when they should be training).
Increased funding to pay for access to high-quality training support and specialist equipment etc.	Inequality of funding means performers in 'minority sports' (e.g. badminton) miss out on funding and full-time professional opportunities.

Table 40 **Positive and negative effects of commercialisation and sponsorship on sport**

Positives	Negatives
Increased funding to a sport to provide improved facilities, equipment, coaching and Talent ID programmes to develop performers in that sport.	Sports might become over-reliant on the funding and income from commercial sources and experience problems if it is withdrawn.
Increased funding to provide technology at events to aid officials' decision making (i.e. reach correct decisions at key times of an event).	Money goes to already popular sports (i.e. there are inequalities of funding, so sports like football are highly attractive to sponsors, while sports such as hockey and trampolining are not).
Increased number of positive role models in a sport to inspire others to take part and increase participation rates in that sport.	The sport sometimes loses control (e.g. ticket allocations at major sports events go to corporate organisations/hospitality as opposed to the 'true fans').
Increased spectator interest and involvement (e.g. via wearing team kit/team colours).	Traditionalists might be against new competitions, rule changes or changes in a sports format to suit the demands of sponsors for more excitement and more breaks for adverts.
Increased number of events and competitions to help generate interest and promote a sport.	The location of events may be influenced by commercial considerations (e.g. American Football matches at Wembley Stadium to help the global appeal of the game).

Exam tips

■ Note that this topic needs to be considered in relation to the five identified groups of performer, coach, official, audience and sport. These are likely to differ considerably.

■ The relationship between sport and the media is a constantly changing and evolving one, so remember to take this into account and keep up to date with current issues.

Do you know?

1 What is meant by the term 'commercialisation'?
2 What three bodies make up the golden triangle?

6.8 Role of technology

You need to know

- understanding of technology for sports analytics
- functions of sports analytics
- the development of equipment and facilities in physical activity and sport, and their impact on participation and performance
- the role of technology in sport and its positive and negative impacts

Synoptic link

The role of technology has a link to Section 4, most notably to preparation and training methods.

Understanding technology

Technology is used in sport to collect and analyse a variety of data for a variety of reasons. This data is commonly used to study the effectiveness of performance. The key terms you need to be aware of relating to data include:

- **quantitative data:** data that can be written down or measured factually, precisely and numerically, e.g. a fitness test score
- **qualitative data:** data that is descriptive and looks at the way people think or feel, e.g. an opinion
- **objective data:** fact-based information which is measurable and usable, e.g. the level achieved on the multi-stage fitness test which links to a VO_2 max score
- **subjective data:** based on personal opinion, which is less measurable and often less usable
- **validity:** an indication of whether the data collected actually measures what it claims to measure
- **reliability:** refers to the degree to which data collection is consistent and stable over time. Reliable tests can be repeated to provide similar data

Note that quantitative data is objective in nature, while qualitative data is subjective in nature.

Exam tip

If we use the example of a fitness test, the score recorded is objective, quantitative data. An opinion about the success or otherwise of the performance is subjective, qualitative data.

Video and analysis programmes

Video and analysis programmes such as video motion analysis, involve a technique used to get information about moving objects from video. Frame by frame analysis may be possible as well as playback and tracking of objects.

Testing and recording equipment

Table 41

Term	Description and purpose
Metabolic cart	■ a device which works by attaching headgear to a subject while the person breaths a specific amount of oxygen over a period of time ■ used for indirect calorimetry
Indirect calorimetry	■ the measurement of the heat and energy generated in an oxidation reaction ■ determined by the amount of oxygen consumed and the amount of carbon dioxide eliminated ■ used to determine RER, which can be used to estimate the RQ ■ also used to calculate REE
Use of GPS	■ navigation system which uses satellites to provide location and time information as well as motion tracking ■ thus, the speed, distance, direction and movement of performers can be tracked and analysed
Maintaining data integrity	■ the data which is gathered must be maintained and those using it must ensure the accuracy and consistency of stored data over its entire lifetime ■ can be compromised by human error, software viruses and disc errors

Functions of sports analytics

The main functions of sports analytics are:
■ to monitor fitness for performance
■ skill and technique development
■ injury prevention (vibration, electro-stimulation)
■ to allow game analysis
■ to assist with talent identification/scouting

Development of equipment and facilities

Technology is ever-advancing and allows new and better ways to adapt equipment and analysis methods for all types of people. Participation rates can therefore increase and performance levels can improve.

- equipment can be adapted for the elderly, e.g. low-impact resistance machines
- equipment can be adapted for performers with disabilities, e.g. prosthetic limbs and lightweight wheelchairs for basketball
- facilities allow for all-weather participation, e.g. 3G pitches, 4G pitches, multi-use facilities etc.
- part of the 'Olympic legacy' from 2012 is the promise to increase participation by providing sports facilities for the local community

Positive and negative effects

Although technology would appear to be a good thing for all parties involved in sport, there are both positive and negative effects (Table 42).

Table 42

Individual/group	Positives	Negatives
Sport	<ul><li>increased participation</li><li>more inclusive</li><li>improved performance</li><li>quality of facilities</li></ul>	<ul><li>expensive</li><li>data can be misleading</li><li>too reliant on data</li></ul>
Performer	<ul><li>improved performance</li><li>improved equipment</li><li>quicker recovery</li><li>analysis of performance</li><li>fairer decisions from officials</li></ul>	<ul><li>may encourage drug-taking</li><li>expensive</li><li>not available to all</li><li>may not like new equipment</li></ul>
Coach	<ul><li>analyse performance</li><li>monitor many variables affecting performance</li><li>aim to provide better equipment</li></ul>	<ul><li>need to understand the technology</li><li>may become over-reliant</li><li>expensive</li></ul>
Audience	<ul><li>watch better performance</li><li>access to information</li><li>increased excitement through watching/hearing decisions</li><li>fairer decisions from officials</li></ul>	<ul><li>changes nature of the sport</li><li>can cause breaks in play</li><li>may be hard to understand</li></ul>

Exam tips

- The positive and negative impacts of technology are likely to be the focal point for any questions relating to this topic. As with the previous topic, this is also going to be linked to the sport, performer, coach or audience.
- This is a topic which is constantly evolving and developing, so it is vital to keep up to date with advances in technology.

Do you know?

1 What is objective data?
2 What is subjective data?
3 How does technology positively affect performers?
4 What is GPS?
5 What is reliable data?

End of section 6 questions

1 State three differences between physical recreation and sport.

2 Which sporting organisation
- develops high-performance sport in the UK?
- aims to increase sporting excellence?

3 What is the Olympic Oath?

4 State the strategies employed to prevent hooliganism.

5 What are the positive and negative effects of media coverage on performers?

6 What are the positive and negative effects of technology on sport?